START: The Sound and Writing Systems of Russian

Second Edition

Аа Бб Вв Гг Дд Ее
Ёё Жж Зз Ии Йй Кк
Лл Мм Нн Оо Пп Рр
Сс Тт Уу Фф Хх Цц
Чч Шш Щщ Ъъ Ыы
Ьь Ээ Юю Яя

Аа Бб Вв Гг Дд Ее
Ёё Жж Зз Ии Йй Кк
Лл Мм Нн Оо Пп Рр
Сс Тт Уу Фф Хх Цц
Чч Шш Щщ Ъъ Ыы
Ьь Ээ Юю Яя

Benjamin Rifkin

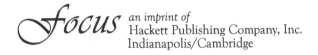
focus an imprint of
Hackett Publishing Company, Inc.
Indianapolis/Cambridge

START
© 2005 Benjamin Rifkin

Previously published by Focus Publishing/R. Pullins Company

Focus an imprint of
Hackett Publishing Company, Inc.
P.O. Box 44937
Indianapolis, Indiana 46244-0937

www.hackettpublishing.com

ISBN-13: 978-1-58510-132-0

Acknowledgments: The author thanks **Kathleen Scollins and Brian Johnson** for their careful editing work and **Anna Tumarkin, David Vernikov, Nikolai Isayev, Anastasia Vener, and Nina Familiant** for giving voice to the words and sounds of the lessons in this manual and/or for demonstrating their excellent penmanship. **Galina Patterson provided the writing samples in the video files in the courseware.** Thanks also to **Doug Worsham** of the UW-Madison Learning Support Services for his great help in the recording studio and to **Bruno Browning, Karen Tusack** and **Mary Prochniak** of LSS for their help with these materials as well. Funding for this project was provided in part by the UW-Madison **Center for Russia, Eastern Europe and Central Asia.**

Note to Students: Be sure to read the Preface before you start working with Lesson 1!

Note to Instructors: For more information on courseware (i.e., audio and video files available for separate purchase), keys to self-quizzes and dictations, as well as sample self-quizzes, visit our website, www.hackettpublishing.com.

Instructors interested in acquiring a site license should contact faculty@hackettpublishing.com.

Table of Contents

Introduction

As a fluent speaker of English, you know that the English alphabet has 26 letters. You may think that each one of those 26 letters has a single and specific sound. However, this is far from the case. Consider this sentence:

Even through the grey cement walls, Ginger, Gary and I could hear the ghosts laughing.

Consider the letter "g" and the sound it makes in the following words: through, **grey**, **G**inger, **G**ary, **g**hosts, lau**g**hing. This one letter can convey many different sounds and can even be silent. Students of English as a second language find the lack of correspondence between the writing and sound systems of English extremely challenging. Teachers of English as a second language joke that the word "fish" can be spelled "ghoti" as follows:

gh as in cou**gh**
o as in w**o**men
ti as in infla**ti**on

As a fluent speaker of English, you are very used to the very idiosyncratic rules of English spelling and pronunciation. The Russian alphabet, with its 33 letters, may seem challenging to you. However, the Russian language has very clear and systematic rules for spelling and pronunciation. Countless American university students learn the Russian alphabet in just a week or so and you can, too.

Before we begin, it's good to review some basic concepts that we'll be referring to frequently in our study of the sound and writing systems of Russian. When we refer to letters, we use the quotation marks around the letter to indicate that. When we refer to the sounds those letters create, we use vertical lines, such as |m| to indicate just the sound the letter represents .

> **Consonant letter:** a *letter* of the alphabet representing a consonant sound, such as, in English, the letters "g" or "m" or "k"
>
> **Consonant sound:** any *sound* made by a partial or complete obstruction of the flow of air through the speech organs, such as the sounds |g|, |m|, |z| or |k|
>
> **Vowel letter:** a *letter* of the alphabet representing a vowel sound, such as, in English, the letters "a", "e", "i", "o", or "u" (and sometimes "y")
>
> **Vowel sound:** a *sound* made by the unrestricted flow of air through the speech organs, such as |a|, |o|, |u|, and the like.

In order for you to learn the Russian sound and writing system efficiently, we will teach you the letters of the alphabet in 5 groups of 6-7 letters each. In each odd-numbered lesson 1-9, we will teach you first how to read and pronounce the Cyrillic letters in romanface and *italics*. In the even-numbered lessons, you'll learn how to recognize and write in cursive those letters presented in the immediately preceding odd-numbered lesson. Using the Russian cursive script is essential because Russians never "write" in "print letters" the way Americans sometimes do. Print letters are reserved only for publication; cursive is the style that all Russians use when they take pen to hand. In Lesson 11, you'll learn how to pronounce the multisyllabic Russian words. The Appendix consists of summaries of some of the important information that is built up in each of the first ten lessons and some information about the alphabetical order in Russian.

Audio Files: The audio files for this book are in mp3 format and may be found in the courseware available for purchase at www.hackettpublishing.com. Audio files for every lesson are included, by lesson, in the courseware. The numbered audio files correspond to the numbered sections of the lessons in these manuals that have an audio file for you to listen to. Listening to the audio files will help you master the fundamentals of Russian pronunciation. As you listen, you'll hear a male and female pronounce each sound. The two native speakers may, at times, seem to pronounce the sounds differently. Be assured that in such instances where the pronunciations seem to differ, in fact both pronunciations are within the range of normative Russian pronunciation. You should try to pronounce the sounds close to one of the samples you hear.

Video Files: The video files in the courseware correspond only to the even-numbered lessons of this book. These video files can be played on both Windows and Macintosh computers with the QuickTime plug-in. The video files depict the writing of the cursive letters of the Russian alphabet in various combinations (each letter in word-initial, mid-word, and word-final position with a variety of other letters before and after it). There are video files for most, *but not all*, of the writing samples in this manual. Your goal is to watch the video files as much as you need to to learn how to write the letters of the cursive alphabet; test yourself with the letter combinations which do not have corresponding video files. Above all, watch the video files to improve your ability to write Russian letters in the Russian cursive script and to improve your understanding of written Russian. When in Russia, you'll need to be able to "decipher" handwritten notes from your friends, acquaintances, co-workers, colleagues, clients, and customers.

Note: The following courseware files are no longer active: 8.3.2, 8.7.16, 10.1.3, 10.7.3, 10.9.13.

Learning Tips:

(1) Learn to recognize and pronounce the Russian letters in Russian. *Don't try to transcribe the letters into English sounds*. That will only delay your learning process.

(2) The sounds presented throughout these lessons are, for the most part, *not words*. They are the building blocks of Russian words. Occasionally, one of the sound combinations in the lessons is actually a word and in most of those cases, that word is illustrated. It is NOT your responsibility to master that vocabulary now. The purpose of this manual is to teach you how to understand and use the sound and writing systems of Russian, not to learn vocabulary. Your teacher will tell you if any of the words in this manual are, in fact, required vocabulary.

Lesson 1

This lesson introduces 7 letters of the Russian alphabet. Some of these letters may look familiar to you because they look like letters in the English alphabet and, in some cases, may be pronounced in ways that seem similar to the English alphabet. By the end of this lesson, you'll be able to recognize and read out loud the Russian abbreviation USSR (which stands for "The Union of Soviet Socialist Republics") as well as a number of other Russian words.

New Letters

This lesson presents to you 7 Russian letters. Of these seven letters, two are vowel letters and five are consonant letters. The letters will be presented in a sequence that makes pedagogical sense, not in the order in which they occur in the alphabet. However, to start you off, here is the Russian alphabet, with the letters of Lesson 1 underlined:

Аа Бб Вв Гг Дд Ее Ёё Жж Зз Ии Йй Кк Лл Мм Нн Оо Пп
Рр Сс Тт Уу Фф Хх Цц Чч Шш Щщ Ъъ Ыы Ьь Ээ Юю Яя

1.1   Аа *Aa* (1.1 = audio file number)

The first letter of Lesson 1 is the first letter of the Russian alphabet. Just as in English, this letter represents a vowel sound. In Russian, this is considered a hard-series vowel. (Trust us for now; we'll explain more what this means before the end of this lesson.) When this letter occurs in a word of only one-syllable, it is always pronounced in a way that rhymes with the English words "pot" or "cot" in midwestern American (not British) pronunciation. When the letter occurs in words of longer than one syllable, the pronunciation will vary according to the rules that will be presented in lesson 11.

1.2   Тт *Tm* (1.2 = audio file number)

This letter is a voiceless consonant letter. (The term "voiceless" will be explained in section 1.5 below.) It may be a **hard** or **soft consonant**, as will be explained in section 1.7 below. For now, practice pronouncing these letter combinations:

Ат

Та

Am

Ta

The italics version of the lower case may look like another English letter.

Important Note: In the materials presented above and throughout this manual, romanface (Ат) and italics (*Am*) will alternate so that you can learn to recognize both styles of print.

1.3   Сс *Сс*

This letter is another voiceless consonant letter that may represent a hard or soft consonant sound, as will be explained in section 1.7 below. For now, practice these letter combinations:

Сат

Тасс

Аст

Атс

Тса

Сат

Тасс

Аст

Атс

Тса

1.4   Рр *Рр*

This letter is a voiced consonant (see section 1.5) known as a liquid. It is "rolled" or "trilled" as you might expect to hear it in Spanish or Italian, rather than French or German. It, too, may be hard or soft, as will be explained in section 1.7.

1.4.1

Рат

Рас

Тра

Сар

Тар

Сарт

Старт

Трас

Рат

Рас

Тра

Сар

Тар

Сарт

Трас

Старт

1.4.2　ТР тр

It's very important to note that in English, the combination "tr" is often pronounced like |chr| as in the words "train" or "tree". In Russian, the combination "тр" is never pronounced with a "ch" sound. Practice with these combinations:

Тра

Трас

Тра

Трас

1.4.3

Now that you've learned this letter, you can recognize and pronounce the abbreviation USSR:

CCCP

1.5　Зз *Зз*

Some of the consonant letters thus far have been marked as "voiceless". But what does that mean? It means that the consonant sounds they represent are created without the vibration of the vocal cords. Put the palm of your hand on your throat and pronounce the woman's name "Sue". Now, keeping the palm of your hand on your throat, pronounce the English word "zoo". You should feel a vibration in your throat when you pronounce "zoo," but not when you pronounce "Sue." That's because |s| is a voiceless consonant sound, but |z| is a voiced consonant sound. This is an important distinction because Russian has a pronunciation rule called

The rule of regressive assimilation

This is a big phrase that means simply that the pronunciation of one consonant is influenced by the consonant that follows it.

1.5.1   Сс / Зз

In Russian, there are many pairs of consonants, each pair consisting of a voiced and voiceless consonant. One of these pairs is С / З.

Practice with these sounds:

Зат

Зас

Зра

Зар

Зарт

Зрас

Зат

Зас

Зра

Зар

Зарт

Зрас

Here is a very important rule about voiced and voiceless consonants:

In word-final position, a voiced consonant is pronounced like its voiceless mate.

1.5.2   Voiced consonants in word-final positions

Each pair of letter combinations below (in the same row) is pronounced *the same*: there is no difference in their pronunciation.

Тас	Таз
Рас	Раз
Зас	Заз
Трас	Траз
Зрас	Зраз
Тас	*Таз*
Рас	*Раз*
Зас	*Заз*
Трас	*Траз*
Зрас	*Зраз*

1.6　　Дд *Дд*

This is another voiced consonant (like Зз). Its voiceless mate is Тт. Like the letters Сс and Тт, it can also be a hard or soft consonant (see section 1.7). Remember, in word-final position, Дд will be pronounced like Тт. Note that the lower-case italic form of this letter looks different from the other versions of the letter: it has a spine that rises up and "bends" to the left. This is an important detail that will help you distinguish this form of the letter from another letter whose spine rises up and bends to the right.

1.6.1

Да		*means "YES"*
Дас	Даз	
Дра		
Драс	Драз	
Драт	Драд	
Дар		*means "gift" or "talent" - the title of a novel by Nabokov*
Рат	Рад	
Сат	Сад	
Зат	Зад	
Дас	*Даз*	
Дар		
Дра		
Драс	*Драз*	
Драт	*Драд*	
Рат	*Рад*	
Сат	*Сад*	
Зат	*Зад*	

1.6.2　СД сд

When Дд is preceded by the voiceless consonant Сс, the voiceless consonant Сс is pronounced like Зз! This is another example of the rule of regressive assimilation. Practice with these combinations; each row presents contrasting sounds:

Стар	Сдар
Стра	Сдра
Ста	Сда
Стар	*Сдар*
Стра	*Сдра*

Ста   Сда

1.7   Яя *Яя*

The last letter of this lesson is the last letter of the Russian alphabet. This letter is a soft-series vowel. If you've been wondering about the references to hard and soft consonants in sections 1.2 through 1.6, now you'll get your answer.

All Russian consonants can be divided into three categories based on the way they are pronounced. In one category we have consonants that are always "hard". (There are only three such consonants and you haven't learned any of them just yet.) In another category we have consonants that are always "soft". (There are only three of those and you haven't learned them yet, either.) The rest of the consonants of the Russian alphabet may be hard or soft depending on the letter that follows them. (This is another example of the rule of regressive assimilation.)

A soft consonant is either:

➤ One of the three consonants that is always soft (you'll learn them later)
➤ A consonant that is followed by a soft-series vowel (such as Яя)
➤ A consonant that is followed by a soft-sign (you'll learn that in lesson 9)

A hard consonant is either:

➤ One of the three consonants that is always hard (you'll learn them later)
➤ A consonant that is followed by a hard-series vowel (such as Аа)
➤ A consonant that is followed by a hard-sign (you'll learn that in lesson 9)
➤ A consonant that is not always soft and is in word-final position

The pronunciation of a consonant that can be either hard or soft depends on the pronunciation of the letter that follows it. When we use the terms "hard" and "soft" we are referring to the nature of the pronunciation of the sound. The pronunciation is determined by the placement of the tongue in the mouth when the sound is pronounced.

When the consonants are soft, they are pronounced by the middle of the tongue touching upper soft palate (the soft part of the roof of your mouth). The tendency in English is to pronounce sounds at the front of the mouth, so this will be a challenge for you at first. Practice it now, even if it makes you feel self-conscious, until it becomes easy for you to do without thinking about.

Practice listening to and repeating the sounds below:

1.7.1

Initial Soft Consonant	**Initial Hard Consonant**
Тяс	Тас
Тяр	Тар
Тят	Тат
Сяс	Сас
Сяр	Сар
Сят	Сат

Зяс	Зас
Initial Soft Consonant	**Initial Hard Consonant**
Зяр	Зар
Зят	Зат
Дяс	Дас
Дяр	Дар
Дят	Дат
Ряс	Рас
Ряр	Рар
Рят	Рат
Зря	Зра
Дря	Дра
Тря	Тра

1.7.2 Яя and the **y-glide**

The soft-series vowel Яя has a special characteristic. When it is in word-initial position, it is pronounced with a "y-glide" as in the word "yawn" or "yes". Practice with these combinations; the sounds in each row are DIFFERENT.

Яс	Ас	
Яр	Ар	
Ят	Ат	
Яд	Ад	*the first means "poison", the second means "hell"*
Яз	Аз	
Яс	*Ас*	
Яр	*Ар*	
Ям	*Ам*	
Яд	*Ад*	*the first means "poison", the second means "hell"*
Яз	*Аз*	

Summary Practice

1.8   Practice pronouncing the letter combinations below. Remember that voiced consonants in word final position are pronounced as their voiceless mates. Some of the words are in Italics in order to give you practice reading and recognizing the Italic letters.

1. Тра	15. *Старт*	29. Раз	*43. Ряст*
2. Дра	16. *Зря*	*30. Драс*	*44. Рязд*
3. Сат	17. Сра	31. Драз	*45. Яр*
4. Сяд	18. Рат	32. Тарт	*46. Ар*
5. Дас	*19. Рад*	33. Тарс	*47. Ас*
6. Даз	20. *Рас*	*34. Тарз*	48. Яс
7. Рас	21. Раз	35. Зарт	49. Ат
8. Раз	22. Дар	36. Сарт	*50. Яд*
9. Драс	*23. Тар*	37. Стра	*51. Стра*
10. Дряс	24. *Сар*	*38. Здра*	52. Сдра
11. Дряз	25. Дат	*39. Драз*	*53. Стар*
12. *Тряс*	*26. Дад*	*40. Дряз*	*54. Сдар*
13. Трас	27. *Тас*	*41. Раст*	*55. Сдяр*
14. Траз	28. Рас	*42. Разд*	*56. Стяр*

Self-Quiz

Part 1. Listen to the sounds in the sound file and circle the letter combination that best represents the spelling of that sound.

1	Тар	Трас	Тяс
2	Дар	Дяр	Дас
3	Зат	Зас	Зяд
4	Дра	Дря	Дар
5	Ста	Стя	Стра
6	Раст	Ряст	Рад
7	Аст	Яст	Ат
8	Стар	Сдар	Сдяр
9	Зра	Зря	Стра
10	Рас	Ряз	Трас
11	Ярт	Ард	Дарт
12	Тяс	Тас	Трас
13	Дас	Дяс	Тяс
14	Трас	Тряс	Трат
15	Драс	Дряс	Драт
16	Старт	Сдарт	Сдар
17	Язд	Аст	Ят
18	Дяр	Дяс	Даз
19	Тас	Зас	Тяс
20	Дат	Дят	Дас

Part 2. Circle the letters that best fit the category presented in each question.

1.	Voiced consonants:	С	Т	З	Д	Р
2.	Voiceless consonants:	С	Т	З	Д	Р
3.	Hard-series vowels:	А	Я			
4.	Soft-series vowels:	А	Я			

Considering each combination of letters below, underline the ...

5.	Hard consonants:	Стар	Тяс	Зат	Дяс	Ряд	Тар	Сдяс	Драт
6.	Soft consonants:	Стар	Тяс	Зат	Дяс	Ряд	Тар	Сдяс	Драт

Lesson 2

Congratulations! You've learned to recognize and pronounce seven Russian letters including two vowel letters (Аа, Яя) and five consonant letters (Тт, Сс, Зз, Дд, Рр) in both romanface and Italics. Now you'll learn how to recognize and read those same letters when written in Russian cursive script.

New Letters

2.1   Aa, *Аа*, Cc, *Сс*

These letters are easy to write because they are so similar to the English letters. **The sounds pronounced by the letters below are recorded in the audio file 2.1, as are all the sounds in the even-numbered lessons (which are focused on penmanship.)**

2.1-0a   A   _____ _____

2.1-0b   a   _____ _____

2.1-0c   C   _____ _____

2.1-0d   c   _____ _____

Practice these combinations in your homework (on a separate piece of paper):

2.1-1 Ac   _____ _____

2.1-2 ac   _____ _____

2.1-3 Ca   _____ _____

2.1-4 ca   _____ _____

2.2   Зз *Зз*

The upper-case cursive letter З is written entirely above the line. Practice these combinations in your homework (on a separate piece of paper):

2.2-0a   З   _____ _____

2.2-0b   з   _____ _____

2.2-1 Зac   _____ _____

        зac   _____ _____

Саз   _____   _____

2.2-4   саз   _____   _____

2.3   Рр *Рр*

The lower-case cursive letter р has a loop that does not close at the bottom, unlike the English lower-case letter p. Practice these combinations in your homework (on a separate piece of paper):

2.3-0a   Р   _____   _____

2.3-0b   р   _____   _____

2.3-1   Рас   _____   _____

2.3-2   раз   _____   _____

2.3-3   сар   _____   _____

2.3-4   зар   _____   _____

Зра   _____   _____

Сра   _____   _____

2.3-7   рас   _____   _____

2.3-8   рад   _____   _____

2.4   Дд *Дg*

The lower-case cursive letter д may be written in one of either two ways. One of these looks very much like the italic lowercase *д* (2.4-0c, with a "spine"), while the other looks like an English cursive lower-case *g* (2.40b, with a "tail"). Practice these combinations in your homework (on a separate piece of paper):

2.4-0a   Д   _____   _____

2.4-0b   д (tail)   _____   _____

2.4-0c   д (spine)   _____   _____

2.4-1   Дас   _____   _____

2.4-2   дaz   _____   _____

2.4-3   сад   _____   _____

2.4-4   рад   _____   _____

        Дра   _____   _____

        Сра   _____   _____

        Дра   _____   _____

2.4-8   сдар   _____   _____

2.4-9   дар   _____   _____

2.5   Тт *Тт*

The lower-case cursive letter т may also be written in one of either two ways. One of these looks very much like the italic lowercase *m*, while the other looks more like the lower-case romanface т. Practice these combinations in your homework (on a separate piece of paper):

2.5-0a   Д   _____   _____

2.5-0b   т (with a bar) _____   _____

2.5-0c   т (no bar) _____   _____

        Дат   _____   _____

        дат   _____   _____

2.5-3   тра   _____   _____

        Сат   _____   _____

2.5-4   рат   _____   _____

        арт   _____   _____

        трас   _____   _____

2.5-8   Тар   _____   _____

        та   _____   _____

2.6   Яя *Яя*

Both upper- and lower-case cursive letters **Яя** *must* have a little hook from which the letter is written. (Start writing from the lower left with this hook.) Practice these combinations in your homework (on a separate piece of paper):

2.6-0a   Я   _____ _____

2.6-0b   я   _____ _____

2.6-0a Я   _____ _____

Яд   _____ _____

ят   _____ _____

2.6-4 Яр   _____ _____

яз   _____ _____

Ся   _____ _____

тя   _____ _____

Ряс   _____ _____

ряд   _____ _____

Рят   _____ _____

2.6-11 зря   _____ _____

2.6-12 тря   _____ _____

Сря   _____ _____

тя   _____ _____

Зя   _____ _____

яр   _____ _____

2.6-17 ят   _____ _____

Summary Practice

2.7   Practice I with sound files.

Write out these letters and combinations. Letter combinations marked with an asterisk (*) have corresponding video files 2.7-1, 2.7-2, etc.

1. тяс*   _____   _____

2. тяр*   _____   _____

3. дяс*   _____   _____

4. дяр*   _____   _____

5. Ряс*   _____   _____

6. Старт*   _____   _____

7. драт   _____   _____

8. дряс   _____   _____

9. Ряст   _____   _____

10. Рязд   _____   _____

11. Тар*   _____   _____

12. Тас*   _____   _____

13. Тат   _____   _____

14. дар*   _____   _____

15. Зар   _____   _____

16. Зря   _____   _____

17. зар*   _____   _____

18. Зат   _____   _____

19. Зас*   _____   _____

20. таз*   _____   _____

21. раз*   _____   _____

22. ряз*   _____   _____

23. Раст   _____   _____

24. Драс   _____   _____

25. Здрас   _____   _____

2.9   Practice II

Practice these letter combinations: the sound file is start2-9.mp3; the video files are 2.9-1, 2.9-2, etc.

1. аз*   _____   _____

2. ад*   _____   _____

3. дас*   _____   _____

4. Дяр*   _____   _____

5. Дяд*   _____   _____

6. дят*   _____   _____

7. ряд*   _____   _____

8. стар*   _____   _____

9. старт*   _____   _____

10. сяр*   _____   _____

11. таз*   _____   _____

12. За*   _____   _____

13. здар*   _____   _____

14. зяр*   _____   _____

Dictation

2.9   Dictation

Listen to the tape and write out the sounds you hear in Cyrillic cursive letters. If it is possible to write the same sound combination in more than one different way, due to rules governing voiced and voiceless consonants, the sound will recur in two successive dictation items. In that case, be sure to write it out in two different spellings. There are a total of 20 items.

Lesson 3

In Lessons 1-2 you learned to recognize, pronounce and write 7 Russian letters, including two vowel letters and 5 consonant letters. Two pairs of the consonant letters (Дд/Тт, Зз/Сс) are pairs of voiced and voiceless consonant letters; one consonant letter (Рр) is an unpaired voiced consonant. All of the consonants introduced in Lessons 1-2 may be either hard or soft. One of the vowels introduced in Lessons 1-2 was a hard-series vowel (Аа), while the other is a soft-series vowel (Яя). In lesson 3, you will learn to recognize and pronounce 7 more Russian letters, including two more vowel letters and 5 more consonant letters. But first, let's review.

Review

Remember, there are three groups of consonant letters in Russian:

1) consonants that are <u>always hard</u> (none presented so far)
2) consonants that are <u>always soft</u> (none presented so far)
3) consonants that may be <u>either hard or soft</u>, depending on the phonetic context (all the consonants presented in lessons 1-2)

Consonants of group 3 are hard if:

- Followed by another hard consonant or a hard-series vowel (Аа)
- Word-final
- Followed by the hard-sign (see Lesson 9)

Consonants of group 3 are soft if:

- Followed by another soft consonant or a soft-series vowel (Яя)
- Followed by the soft-sign (see Lesson 9)

3.1   Hard and Soft Consonants

In each pair of sound combinations below, the first pair features a **hard** word-initial consonant, while the second pair features a **soft** word initial consonant. Each pair of sound combinations, in a given row, represents a significant contrast in the word-initial consonant: hard vs. soft.

Рас	Ряс
Раз	Ряз
Зар	Зяр
Дар	Дяр
Сат	Сят
Сад	Сяд

3.2 Each pair of sound combinations in the same row below is **pronounced identically, even though they are spelled differently**. Remember that voiced consonants in word-final position are pronounced as if they were their voiceless mate.

Рас	Раз
Ряс	Ряз
Зат	Зад
Зят	Зяд
Ас	Аз
Ят	Яд
Раст	Разд
Ряст	Рязд
Старт	Стард

3.3 When the voiceless consonant is followed by a voiced consonant, remember that it is pronounced like its voiced mate. The sounds below in the same row are **pronounced the same, even though they are spelled differently**.

Сдар	Здар
Сдра	Здра
Сдрас	Здрас
Сдряс	Здряс

New Letters

In this lesson you will learn 7 new Russian letters. They are presented in an order that makes pedagogical sense, but not in alphabetical order. Here are the letters of the Russian alphabet with the letters of Lesson 3 underscored:

Аа <u>Бб</u> Вв <u>Гг</u> Дд Ее Ёё Жж Зз Ии Йй <u>Кк</u> Лл <u>Мм</u> Нн Оо <u>Пп</u>
Рр Сс Тт <u>Уу</u> Фф Хх Цц Чч Шш Щщ Ъъ Ыы Ьь Ээ <u>Юю</u> Яя

3.4   Пп *Пп*

The letter Пп *Пп* may remind you of a Greek symbol you may have used in math class to discuss the area of a circle. This consonant is always voiceless, but it may be hard or soft. The first set of sounds in each row features a hard word-initial consonant, while the second set of sounds in each row below features a soft word-initial consonant.

Hard Пп	Soft Пп
Пас	пяс
Пат	*пят*
Пар	пяр
Паз	*пяз*
Пра	пря

3.5   Be sure to distinguish between Russian Пп and Рр. Practice these sound combinations:

Рап	Ряп
Ап	*Яп*
Ар	Арп
Тап	*Сап*
Рат	Рап
Спа	*Спя*
Спра	Спря

3.6   Кк *Кк*

The Russian letter Кк is a voiceless consonant (its voiced mate will be presented later) that may be hard or soft. It is the first consonant presented thus far that is affected by the spelling rules of Russian. This consonant can never be followed by the soft-series vowel Яя. This means, for the time being, that you will only see Кк as a hard consonant, but instances of Кк as a soft consonant will be presented in later lessons. For now practice with these sounds

Кар	Кат	
Кас	*Каз*	
Раск	Скра	
Так		*means "thus" or "so"*
Как		*means "how"*
Кад	*Пак*	
Парк		*means "park" (noun)*
Рак		*means "crab"*
Зак		

Рак

3.7 Мм *Мм*

The Russian letter Мм is a voiced consonant (without a voiceless mate) that may be hard or soft. The first set of sounds in each row features a hard word-initial consonant, while the second set of sounds in each row below features a soft word-initial consonant.

Hard Мм	Soft Мм	
Мас	мяс	
Мат	*мят*	
Мар	мяр	
Маз	*мяз*	
Мра	мря	
Март		*means month of "March"*
Марс		*means planet of "Mars"*
Марк		*means man's name "Mark"*

3.8 *Мм / Тт*

Notice that the italic forms of these letters may be a bit confusing in the lower case. Practice them here.

там	*мат*
март	*трам*
арм	*ярт*
мра	*тра*
ям	*ят*
сат	*сам*
срам	*старт*

3.9 Бб *Бб*

Бб is a voiced consonant that may be hard or soft. It's voiceless mate is Пп. In its lower-case italic form, Бб has a spine that rises up and bends to the left. (Distinguish it from lower case italic Дд *Дд*).

Hard Бб	Soft Бб
Бас	Бяс
Баз	*Бяз*
Бар	Бяр

Бар

Бак	*Бяк*
Бам	Бям
Бад	*Бяд*
бас	бяс
баз	*бяз*
бар	бяр
бак	*бяк*
бам	бям
бад	*бяд*

3.10   Бб *Бб* preceded by voiceless consonant Сс

When Бб is preceded by voiceless consonant Сс, the voiceless consonant Сс is pronounced like its voiced mate Зз. Sounds in the same row are pronounced identically even though they have different spellings.

Сба	Зба
Сбя	Збя
Сда	Зда
Сдя	Здя

3.11   Бб *Бб* in word-final position

Because Бб is a voiced consonant, when it is in word-final position, it is pronounced like its voiceless mate Пп. Sounds in the same row are pronounced identically even though they are spelled differently.

Рап	Раб
Ряп	*Ряб*
Мап	Маб
Мяп	*Мяб*
Тап	Таб
Стап	*Стаб*
Трап	Траб
Тряп	*Тряб*

3.12   Гг *Гг*

Гг is a voiced consonant that may be hard or soft. However, like Кк, it too is affected by spelling rules. The soft-series vowel letter Яя may never be written after Гг. Accordingly, for the time being, you will only see the consonant letter Гг in contexts in which it is pronounced hard. Later in these materials (in subsequent lessons), you will learn contexts in which Гг is soft.

Гар

Гат

Гам

Гас

Грам

Грас

Град

гар

гат

гам

гас

грам

грас

град

3.13   Гг *Гг* in word-final position

Because Гг is a voiced consonant, when it is in word-final position, it is pronounced like its voiceless mate Кк. Sounds in the same row are pronounced identically even though they are spelled differently.

Паг	Пак
Пяг	Пяк
Баг	Бак
Бяг	Бяк
Маг	Мак
Мяг	Мяк
Таг	Так
Тяг	Тяк
Стаг	Стак
Стяг	Стяк

3.14 Гг *Гг* preceded by voiceless consonant Сс

When Гг is preceded by voiceless consonant Сс, the voiceless consonant Сс is pronounced like its voiced mate Зз. Sounds in the same row are pronounced identically even though they have different spellings.

Сга	Зга
Сда	Зда
Сба	Зба
Сдя	Здя
Сбя	Збя

(Remember, due to spelling rules, Гг cannot be followed by Яя.)

3.15 Уу *Уу*

The hard-series vowel Уу is pronounced very differently from its English "cousin" Uu. In order to pronounce the Russian sound correctly, you must extend your lips as far as you can from your face. If you are pronouncing the sound correctly, you should be able to see your lips when you look down toward your mouth. Listen and practice with these examples:

Ус

Ум

Ут

Ук

Уп

Ур

Уз

ус

ум

ут

ук

уп

ур

уз

Ум

3.16   More practice with Уу

Пук

Пуг

Бук

Буг

Муп

Муб

Гуп

Губ

пук

пуг

бук

буг

муп

муб

гуп

губ

3.17   Юю *Юю*

The Russian vowel letter Юю *Юю* is a soft-series vowel. To pronounce it correctly, you must extend your lips fully, just as you do with the pronunciation of Уу. Practice with these sounds:

Мюс

Мюз

Мюк

Мюг

Рюс

Рюз

Рюк

Рюг

Тюк

Тюг

Тюс

Тюз

Тюм

3.18　Юю and the y-glide

The soft-series vowel Юю has a y-glide just like Яя when it is in word-initial position. Practice with these combinations; the sounds in each row are DIFFERENT.

Яс	Ас
Яр	Ар
Ят	Ат
Юп	Уп
Юк	Ук
Ют	Ут
Юс	Ус
Юр	Ур
Яс	*Ас*
Яр	*Ар*
Ят	*Ат*
Юп	*Уп*
Юк	*Ук*
Ют	*Ут*
Юс	*Ус*
Юр	*Ур*
Юг	*Юк*

3.19　Spelling Rules

Neither soft-series vowel Ю, nor soft-series vowel Я may be written after Г or К.

To summarize, after Г or К, never write Ю or Я.

Summary Practice

3.20   Practice these sounds as a review for all the sounds and letters of Lessons 1-3.

1. Паст	14. дюб	27. Мюк	40. сюд
2. Пазд	15. мук	28. мюг	41. зум
3. пак	16. Муг	29. стам	42. зюм
4. паг	17. Тум	30. стям	43. Ум
5. руп	18. Тюм	31. сгам	44. Юм
6. руб	19. Рап	32. згам	45. Ар
7. дуп	20. ряп	33. Сдам	46. Яр
8. Дуб	21. драп	34. Сдям	47. Прук
9. Гуск	22. драб	35. Сбук	48. Прюк
10. Гузг	23. кут	36. Збуг	49. Парк
11. Каск	24. куд	37. Сдют	50. Пярк
12. казг	25. Мяб	38. здют	
13. дюп	26. Мяп	39. суд	

Self-Quiz

Part 1. Listen to the sounds in the sound file and circle the letter combination that best represents the spelling of that sound.

1	Стум	Сдум	Стюм
2	Спак	Сбак	Спяк
3	Грум	Грам	Грюм
4	Брат	Брят	Бяд
5	Каск	Каст	Гаск
6	Траск	Тряск	Тряз
7	Ют	Юм	Ут
8	Юг	Уг	Юп
9	Мут	Мют	Муг
10	Спум	Сбум	Сбюм
11	Трум	Трюм	Трут
12	Пак	Пяк	Пяр
13	Рак	Пак	Пяк
14	Страк	Сдраг	Здряк
15	Скат	Сгат	Стаг
16	Зру	Зрю	Зря
17	Ус	Юз	Ук
18	Труп	Трук	Трюб
19	Спа	Спя	Сбя
20	Так	Тяг	Тюг

Part 2. Circle the letters that best fit the category presented in each question.

1.	Voiced consonants:	П	Б	К	Г	М
2.	Voiceless consonants:	П	Б	К	Г	М
3.	Hard-series vowels:	У	Ю			
4.	Soft-series vowels:	У	Ю			

Considering each combination of letters below, underline the …

5.	Hard consonants:	Драм	Друг	Куз	Пяк	Бюг	Стюм	Сбяр
6.	Soft consonants:	Драм	Друг	Куз	Пяк	Бюг	Стюм	Сбяр

Lesson 4

Congratulations! You've learned to recognize and pronounce seven new Russian letters in Lesson 3 including two vowel letters (Уу Юю) and five consonant letters (Пп, Бб,Кк, Гг, Мм) in both romanface and Italics. Now you'll learn how to recognize and read those same letters when written in Russian cursive script.

Review

4.1   Review

Write out these letter combinations to review how they are written in cursive. **(Remember, you can hear the sounds in audio file 4.1; all the sounds in the even-numbered lessons are recorded for you to practice your phonetics.)**

4.1-1   Старт _____   _____

            Сдяр _____   _____

4.1-3   Зас _____   _____

4.1-4   таз _____   _____

4.1-5   ряд _____   _____

4.1-6   Яр _____   _____

4.1-7   дят _____   _____

4.1-8   аз _____   _____

New Letters

4.2   Пп *Пп*

Practice these combinations:

4.2-0a   П   _____   _____

4.2-0b   п   _____   _____

            Пас   _____   _____

            Асп   _____   _____

4.2-3   рап   _____   _____

4.2-4   пар   _____   _____

4.3   Бб *Бб*

Note that the vertical stroke or spine of the lower-case letter Бб *Бб* turns to the right. Remember
Б: right ("bright"). Practice these combinations:

4.2-0a Б   _____   _____

4.2-0b б   _____   _____

4.3-1   Бар   _____   _____

4.3-2   раб   _____   _____

4.3-3   баз   _____   _____

4.3-4   ряб   _____   _____

4.4   Кк *Кк*

Note that the lower-case letter Кк *Кк* must not exceed the mid-line as its English cousin "k"
does. Practice these combinations:

4.4-0a К   _____   _____

4.4-0b к   _____   _____

4.4-1   Кат   _____   _____

4.4-2   рак   _____   _____

4.4-3   Как   _____   _____

4.4-4   бяк   _____   _____

4.5   Гг *Гг*

4.5-0a Г   _____   _____

4.5-0b г   _____   _____

4.5-1   Габ   _____   _____

4.5-2   Газ   _____   _____

4.5-3   раг   _____   _____

4.5-4   бяг   _____   _____

4.6   Мм *М.м*

Just like Яя, both the upper- and lower-case forms of this letter must have a little hook at the lower left. Start writing the letter from this hook in the lower left.

4.6-0a М   _____   _____

4.6-0b м   _____   _____

4.6-1   Мак   _____   _____

        Мяк   _____   _____

4.6-3   там   _____   _____

        Тям   _____   _____

        стам   _____   _____

        Стям   _____   _____

4.7   Уу *Уу*

The tail of the upper-case Уу must **not** descend below the base line. Note that its tail turns to the left.

4.7-0a У   _____   _____

4.7-0b у   _____   _____

4.7-1   Ус   _____   _____

4.7-2   Ум   _____   _____

4.7-3   мус   _____   _____

        Тум   _____   _____

4.7-5   пум   _____   _____

        Прут   _____   _____

4.8   Юю *Юю*

Practice writing this letter in these combinations:

4.8-0a Ю   _____   _____

4.8-0b ю   _____   _____

4.8-1   Юз   _____   _____

4.8-2   Ют   _____   _____

4.8-3   пюс   _____   _____

        Пют   _____   _____

4.8-5   Мюк   _____   _____

4.8-6   Мюг   _____   _____

Summary Practice

4.9   Practice I with sound files: The letter combinations below marked with an asterisk (*) have video files numbered 4.9-1, 4.9-2, etc. The pronunciation of all these letter combinations can be found in audio file start4-9.mp3.

Practice writing out these letter combinations:

1. Куп* _____   _____
2. гум* _____   _____
3. бюр* _____   _____
4. Кум* _____   _____
5. губ* _____   _____
6. бюг* _____   _____
7. мяб* _____   _____
8. гук* _____   _____
9. бюс* _____   _____
10. дуб* _____   _____
11. Паз* _____   _____
12. Бас* _____   _____
13. Бяр* _____   _____
14. бяс* _____   _____
15. Как* _____   _____
16. ряб* _____   _____
17. даб* _____   _____
18. Кат* _____   _____
19. бак* _____   _____
20. рак* _____   _____
21. Ряг _____   _____
22. град _____   _____
23. Гряк _____   _____
24. мят* _____   _____
25. мат* _____   _____
26. Тум _____   _____
27. тюм _____   _____
28. Тям _____   _____
29. сяг* _____   _____

30. Сбаг   _____   _____

31. Юм*   _____   _____

32. юг   _____   _____

33. Ум*   _____   _____

34. Мюг*   _____   _____

35. рюс*   _____   _____

36. рус*   _____   _____

37. Трус   _____   _____

38. друг*   _____   _____

39. Драк   _____   _____

40. парк   _____   _____

4.10   Practice II. Practice writing out the following letter combinations. The sound file is start4-10.mp3; the video files can be found in 4.10-1, 4.10-2, etc.

1. бар*   _____   _____

2. бяр*   _____   _____

3. дук*   _____   _____

4. дяг*   _____   _____

5. дяб*   _____   _____

6. Гак*   _____   _____

7. гап*   _____   _____

8. гар*   _____   _____

9. гуп*   _____   _____

10. Каб*   _____   _____

11. Кап*   _____   _____

12. кас*   _____   _____

13. каск*   _____   _____

14. казг*   _____   _____

15. Маг*   _____   _____

16. мад*   _____   _____

17. мат*   _____   _____

18. муг*   _____   _____

19. мук*   _____   _____

20. Мур*   _____   _____

21. Мяг* _____   _____

22. Мяр* _____   _____

23. мюг* _____   _____

24. мюк* _____   _____

25. мюс* _____   _____

26. мют* _____   _____

27. пак* _____   _____

28. Пар* _____   _____

29. пур* _____   _____

30. пус* _____   _____

31. пяг* _____   _____

32. пюг* _____   _____

33. рук* _____   _____

34. ряг* _____   _____

35. ряп* _____   _____

36. рюм* _____   _____

37. рюб* _____   _____

38. рюп* _____   _____

39. срам* _____   _____

40. сяб* _____   _____

41. сяп* _____   _____

42. тяг* _____   _____

43. тяк* _____   _____

44. ук* _____   _____

45. Ур* _____   _____

46. Уз* _____   _____

47. Юд* _____   _____

48. сбум* _____   _____

49. збум* _____   _____

50. сгум* _____   _____

Dictation

4.11   Dictation

Listen to the tape and write out the sounds you hear in Cyrillic cursive letters. If it is possible to write the same sound combination in more than one different way, due to rules governing voiced and voiceless consonants, the sound will recur in two successive dictation items. In that case, be sure to write it out in two different spellings. There are a total of 20 items in this dictation.

Lesson 5

You have learned 14 of the 33 letters of the Cyrillic alphabet in Lessons 1-4:

Hard-Series Vowels	А	У
Soft-Series Vowels	Я	Ю

Voiced Consonants	З	Д	Б	Г	Р	М
Voiceless Consonants	С	Т	П	К		

All of the consonants you've learned so far can be hard or soft, although due to the spelling rules, two of the consonant letters (Гг, Кк) that cannot be followed by soft-series vowel Яя have thus far appeared only in contexts in which they are hard. In this lesson you will learn 7 more letters, of which two will be vowel letters and five – consonant letters. Before we go forward, let's review.

Review

Remember, there are three groups of consonant letters in Russian:

1) consonants that are <u>always hard</u> (none presented so far)
2) consonants that are <u>always soft</u> (none presented so far)
3) consonants that may be <u>either hard or soft</u>, depending on the phonetic context (all the consonants presented in lessons 1-4)

Consonants of group 3 are hard if:

- Followed by another hard consonant or a hard-series vowel (Аа, Уу)
- Word-final
- Followed by the hard-sign (see Lesson 9)

Consonants of group 3 are soft if:

- Followed by another soft consonant or a soft-series vowel (Яя, Юю)
- Followed by the soft-sign (see Lesson 9).

5.1   Hard and Soft Consonants

In the sound combinations below, the first pair features a **hard** word-initial consonant, while the second pair features a **soft** word initial consonant.

Бар	Бяр
Пак	*Пяк*
Мук	*Мюк*
Пум	Пюм
Зут	Зют
Сак	*Сяк*

37

5.2   Each pair of sound combinations in the same row below is **pronounced identically, even though they are spelled differently**. Remember that voiced consonants in word-final position are pronounced as if they were their voiceless mate.

Бак	*Баг*	
Зуп	*Зуб*	*the latter means "tooth"*
Пак	*Паг*	
Мук	*Муг*	
Друк	Друг	
Прут	Пруд	
Тяк	*Тяг*	
Рап	*Раб*	

Зуб

5.3   When the voiceless consonant is followed by a voiced consonant, remember that it is pronounced like its voiced mate . The sounds below in the same row are **pronounced the same, even though they are spelled differently**.

Сдар	Здар
Сдра	Здра
Сдрас	Здрас
Сдряс	*Здряс*
Сгар	*Згар*
Сгум	*Згум*
Сграк	Зграк
Сгрюм	Згрюм

New Letters

In this lesson you will learn 7 new letters, of which 2 are vowel letters and 5 are consonant letters. They will be presented in a sequence that makes pedagogical sense, but is not the same as alphabetical order. The letters are presented below, underscored in the Russian alphabet presented in alphabetical order.

Аа Бб Вв Гг Дд <u>Ее</u> Ёё <u>Жж</u> Зз Ии <u>Йй</u> Кк <u>Лл</u> Мм <u>Нн</u> Оо Пп
Рр Сс Тт Уу Фф Хх Цц Чч <u>Шш</u> Щщ Ъъ Ыы Ьь <u>Ээ</u> Юю Яя

5.4   Лл *Лл*

Russian Лл is a voiced consonant (without a voiceless mate) that may be pronounced hard or soft, depending on the phonetic context in which it finds itself.   Listen to these sounds, distinguishing between hard and soft Лл *Лл*.

Hard Лл *Лл*	**Soft Лл *Лл***
Лам	Лям
Лак	Ляк
Лут	*Лют*
Луп	*Люп*
Лар	*Ляр*
Лас	Ляс
Злук	Злюк
Злак	Зляк
Слак	*Сляк*
Слум	*Слюм*

When Лл is preceded by the voiceless consonant Сс, Сс is not affected by the regressive assimilation rule. In other words, although Сс is a voiced consonant, the combination Сл is pronounced |слэ| , not as |зл|.

5.5   Hard Лл *Лл*

Hard Russian Лл is pronounced with the tip of the tongue touching the inside of the upper front teeth. The middle of the tongue is kept low against the floor of the mouth. If it is difficult for you to do this, try sticking your tongue out of your mouth and having the tip of your tongue touch your lip as you pronounce the sound. Then try to achieve the same effect while keeping your tongue in your mouth. Listen and repeat these sounds:

Hard Лл *Лл*

Лам

Лак

Лут

Луп

Лар

Лас

Злук

Злак

Бал

Дул

Зал

Бал

Мул

Мюл

Рал

Кул

5.6   Soft Лл *Лл*

Soft Russian Лл is pronounced not with the tip of the tongue, but with the middle of the tongue!
Let the middle of your tongue gently touch the soft palate of the roof of your mouth. Listen and
repeat these sounds:

Soft Лл *Лл*

Ляп

Лют

Ляр

Лям

Люк

Блюк

Кляк

Скляк

Сляк

Блюс

Люд

Ляб

Лют

Клюк

Слют

Плюм

Блюм

Слят

Плят

Клят

5.7 Contrasting Hard and Soft Лл *Лл*

Listen and practice these sound combinations, distinguishing between hard and soft consonants.

Hard Лл *Лл*	**Soft Лл *Лл***
Лап	Ляп
Лут	Лют
Лар	*Ляр*
Лам	*Лям*
Лук	*Люк*
Лас	Ляс
Лут	Лют
Лук	Люк
Блук	Блюк
Клак	Кляк
Склак	*Скляк*
Слак	*Сляк*
Блус	*Блюс*
Луд	*Люд*
Лаб	Ляб
Лут	Лют
Клук	Клюк
Слут	Слют
Плум	Плюм
Блум	Блюм
Слат	*Слят*
Плат	*Плят*
Клат	*Клят*

the former means "onion"

лук

5.8   Нн *Нн*

Russian Нн is also a voiced consonant (without a voiceless mate) that may be pronounced hard or soft, depending on the phonetic context in which it finds itself.   Listen to these sounds, distinguishing between hard and soft Нн *Нн*.

Hard Нн *Нн*	**Soft Нн *Нн***
Нас	Няс
Нак	*Няк*
Нум	*Нюм*
Нул	*Нюл*
Нар	Няр
Нут	Нют

5.9   Hard Нн *Нн*

Hard Russian Нн is pronounced with the tip of the tongue touching the roof of the mouth at the point where the upper front teeth meet the gums..

Hard Нн *Нн*

Нас

Нак

Нум

Нул

Нар

Нут

Ран

Сан

Кун

Тун

Тюн

Сян

Рун

Тян

5.10   Soft Нн *Нн*

Soft Russian Нн is pronounced with the middle of the tongue touching the soft palate of the roof of the mouth. Think about how the |n| sound in the English words Virginia and California is made in the same way. (Also the child's taunt "nyah-nyah-nyah") or the similar sound in the French word "champagne."

Soft Нн *Нн*

Няк

Нюм

Няр

Няс

Нюп

Нял

Ням

Нют

Нюс

Нюр

5.11   Contrasting Hard and Soft Нн *Нн*

Listen and practice these sound combinations, distinguishing between hard and soft consonants.

Hard Нн *Нн*	**Soft Нн *Нн***
Нап	Няп
Нут	*Нют*
Нар	Няр
Нам	Ням
Нук	*Нюк*
Нут	Нют
Нук	Нюк
Снак	*Сняк*
Снук	Снюк

5.12   Нн *Нн* preceded by Сс

When Нн is preceded by Сс, Сс is not affected by the rule of regressive assimilation. In other words |Сн| is pronounced as |сн|, not as |зн|.

Hard Нн *Нн*	**Soft Нн *Нн***
Снап	Сняп
Снут	Снют
Снар	Сняр
Снам	Сням
Снук	Снюк
Снак	Сняк

5.13   Combinations Нг Нк

In English, the letter combinations "ng" and "nk" are often (but not always) pronounced as a diphthong. That means that the two letters are actually pronounced as one sound (like "sh" in "shall" or "ch" in "child".)   Think about how the letters "ng" and "nk" are pronounced in thiese phrases:

1) They had su**ng** "lasses and lads, come gather ye round."
2) They have new su**ng**lasses.
3) He sure is thi**nk**ing hard.
4) He sure is a thi**n k**ing!

In phrases 1 and 3, the letters "ng" and "nk" are pronounced as one sound for each pair, whereas in phrases 2 and 4 each pair of letters represents two distinct sounds.

In Russian, the letter combinations нг and нк always represent two distinct sounds each. They are *never* diphthongized as in English. Practice with these sound combinations: (Remember, Гг in word-final position is pronounced as its voiceless mate, Кк).

(Audio-file 5.13 begins here.)

Анк

Янк

Ланг

Лянг

Танк

Тянк

Ранг

Рянг

Танк

5.14   Шш *Шш*

The Russian consonant Шш *Шш* is a voiceless consonant (voiced mate to be presented later in this lesson); in this series of lessons it is the first consonant of the group of consonants that is ALWAYS HARD. Like Гг and Кк, it is affected by spelling rules. The soft-series vowels Яя and Юю may never be written after Шш. Always use Аа or Уу. To pronounce this sound correctly, point the tip of your tongue up towards your hard palate (towards the back of the roof of your mouth), without letting the tip of your tongue touch the roof of your mouth. Let the air blow over your tongue and you will be pronouncing the sound correctly. Practice with these sounds:

Шал

Шан

Шак

Наш

Няш

Шур

Руш

Таш

Тяш

Пуш

Шап

Бяш

Люш

Сюш

5.15   Жж *Жж*

The Russian consonant Жж *Жж* is a voiced consonant (its mate is Шш); in this series of lessons it is the second consonant of the group of consonants that is ALWAYS HARD. Like Гг and Кк, it is affected by spelling rules. The soft-series vowels Яя and Юю may never be written after Жж. Always use Аа or Уу. To pronounce this sound correctly, point the tip of your tongue up towards your hard palate (towards the back of the roof of your mouth), without letting the tip of your tongue touch the roof of your mouth. Let the air blow over your tongue and you will be pronouncing the sound correctly. When you do this, you must also vibrate your vocal chords as the air passes through your mouth. Practice with these sounds:

Жал

Жан

Жак

Жур

Жап

Жус

Жут

Жар

Жам

Жум

5.16   Жж *Жж* and Шш *Шш*

These two Russian consonants are called "hushers." Can you tell why? When the voiced consonant is in word-final position, it is pronounced like its voiceless mate, as you have seen before with other pairs of voiced and voiceless consonants. In the combinations of letters below, the sounds in each row are pronounced identically even though they have different spellings.

Лаш	Лаж
Паш	Паж
Няш	*Няж*
Мяш	Мяж
Буш	Буж
Бюш	*Бюш*
Краш	*Краж*
Крюш	*Крюж*
Сташ	*Стаж*
Сбяш	Сбяж

5.17   Combinations Сж (Зж) and Сш (Зш)

When either of the two hushers is preceded by either Сс or Зз, the Сс or Зз is not pronounced. In the combinations of letters below, the sounds in each row are pronounced identically even though they have different spellings.

Сшал	Шал
Сжал	*Жал*
Сшуб	*Шуб*
Сжум	Жум
Зжар	Жар
Зжак	*Жак*

5.18   Йй *Йй*

This letter's name means "short ee". It is a voiced consonant without a voiceless mate and it is the first consonant presented in this series of lessons that is always soft. This consonant letter can never be word-initial in Russian words (although it may appear in word-initial position in the Russian spelling of foreign words, such as "New York"). This letter always follows a vowel letter. Spelling rules of Russian dictate that it is never followed by a vowel and never preceded by a consonant. Listen and practice with these sound combinations:

Ма	Май
Тя	*Тяй*
Жу	*Жуй*
Зю	*Зюй*
Ша	Шай
Ра	Рай
Ля	*Ляй*
Ну	*Нуй*
Там	*Тайм*
Сам	Сайм

5.19   Ээ *Ээ*

The letter Ээ is a hard-series vowel that is rarely used in the middle of words — except for the names of the letters of the alphabet themselves! It is most often used in the beginning of words, especially foreign words borrowed into Russian. Practice with these sounds, all of which are names of letters of the Russian alphabet:

Эл

Эс

Эн

Эр

Эм

Бэ

Гэ

Дэ

Пэ

Жэ

Тэ

Зэ

5.20   Ее *Ee*

The letter Ее is a soft-series vowel that may be pronounced in 4 different ways, depending on the phonetic context in which the letter occurs. For the sake of comparison, American dictionaries typically list 7 or more sounds all spelled with the English letter "e", not including sounds spelled "ea," "ei," "ee," "ey," "ay," and so forth! Each of the four kinds of pronunciation of Russian Ее will be presented in sections 5.21-5.26 below.

5.21   Hard Consonant + Ее + Hard Consonant

In this phonetic pattern, Ее is pronounced like its hard-series mate, Ээ. Note that because Ее is a soft-series vowel, a consonant preceding it will be "softened" unless it is a consonant from the group of consonants that is always hard (Шш, Жж). Practice with these sounds, in which the vowel letters may look different, but are pronounced identically:

Эс

Жес

Эн

Шен

Эт

Шет

Эм

Жем

Эр

Шер

Эк

Жек

Эл

Жел

Эш

Жеш

In addition, some foreign words borrowed into Russian are spelled with Ее but the pronunciation is actually hard: Consider:

Стюардесса

5.22   Soft Consonant + Ee + Hard Consonant

Practice with these sounds, in which the first consonant is soft. Don't insert a y-glide, because there's none there!

Нес

Зес

Нет

Зет

Нел

Зел

Неш

Зеш

Тер

Дер

Тек

Дет

Тем

Дел

Тел

Деш

Лес

Лет

Лел

Нет

| Нет! |

5.23   Ee + Hard Consonant

In this phonetic context, a variant of the context presented in 5.17, there is a y-glide. Practice with these sounds:

Ес	Эс
Ет	*Эт*
Ел	*Эл*
Еш	Эш
Ем	*Эм*
Ер	*Эр*
Ен	Эн

5.24   Hard Consonant + Ee + Soft Consonant

Since you only have two consonants so far that are always hard (Шш, Жж) and only one
consonant that is always soft (Йй), this group has few combinations. Practice with these sounds,
noting the similarity of pronunciation of the vowels in the first and second words, with the vowel
in the third:

Жей

Шей

Эй

5.25   Soft Consonant + Ee + Soft Consonant

Because you only know one consonant that is always soft (Йй), this group is also somewhat
limited.

Лей

Сей

Тей

Бей

Мей

Зей

Пей

Дей

Ней

Рей

Трей

5.26   Ee + Soft Consonant

This is similar to the pronunciation in 5.21, but there is a y-glide.

Ей

5.27   Summary Practice of Vowels Ее and Ээ

1. Эс	2. Ес	3. Эй	4. Ей
5. Шем	*6. Нем*	*7. Шей*	*8. Ней*
9. Шер	10. Тер	11. Жей	12. Зей
13. Жет	14. Дел	15. Шей	16. Тей
17. Шек	*18. Меш*	*19. Жей*	*20. Бей*
21. Жес	22. Блеск	23. Шей	24. Лей

Spelling Rules Updated

Neither soft-series vowel Ю, nor soft-series vowel Я may be written after any of the following letters: Гг, Кк, Шш, Жж.

To summarize, after Гг, Кк, Шш, Жж, never write Ю or Я.

5.28   Soft Гг and Кк

Now that you know soft-series vowel Ее, you can see contexts in which the consonants Гг, Кк are pronounced soft:

Гер

Кер

Геш

Кеш

Ген

Кен

5.29   Же, Ше

Even when followed by soft-series vowel Ее, the hushers Шш, Жж are always hard. When you pronounce them in the following combinations, as you have seen in sections 5.17 and 5.20, it sounds as if you are saying Ээ:

Жек

Шен

Summary Practice

5.30   Practice these sounds as a review for all the sounds and letters of Lessons 1-5.
Remember that voiced consonants in word-final position are pronounced like their voiceless
mates (except for those voiced consonants that are "mateless").

1. Лап	21. Лак	42. Жур	63. Са
2. Ляп	22. Ляг	43. Руш	64. Сайм
3. Лаб	23. Пюш	44. Руж	65. Та
4. Ляб	24. Пюж	45. Ряш	66. Тайм
5. Лут	25. Наг	46. Ряж	67. Жу
6. Лют	26. Нак	47. Жук	68. Жуй
7. Луд	27. Нюп	48. Жуг	69. Бэ
8. Люд	28. Нюб	49. Буш	70. Бес
9. Лек	29. Снар	50. Бюш	71. Бей
10. Лег	30. Сняр	51. Деш	72. Беш
11. Лес	31. Жал	52. Деж	73. Шей
12. Лез	32. Шал	53. Ма	74. Шест
13. Дал	33. Лаш	54. Май	75. Ест
14. Бал	34. Лаж	55. Га	76. Эс
15. Зал	35. Ляш	56. Гай	77. Лет
16. Дул	36. Ляж	57. Жа	78. Лей
17. Мул	37. Шар	58. Жай	79. Лес
18. Дюл	38. Жар	59. Зя	80. Жей
19. Бял	39. Жуб	60. Зяй	
20. Рял	40. Жуп	61. Тю	
	41. Шур	62. Тюй	

Лес

Self-Quiz

Part 1. Listen to the sounds in the sound file and circle the letter combination that best represents the spelling of that sound.

1	Эс	Ес	Ест
2	Шест	Жест	Шеск
3	Лай	Лей	Луй
4	Жан	Жак	Шан
5	Паш	Пяж	Пал
6	Май	Ма	Мяй
7	Тяй	Тя	Тай
8	Нук	Нюк	Нум
9	Тес	Тел	Теж
10	Жуй	Жу	Шу
11	Шам	Жам	Шан
12	Дел	Дал	Дял
13	Шуп	Жуб	Жум
14	Сей	Сел	Ел
15	Нет	Ет	Эт
16	Анк	Танк	Ранг
17	Люм	Лум	Луп
18	Блус	Блюс	Бюст
19	Сшал	Сжал	Шап
20	Эй	Ей	Еш

Part 2. Circle the letters that best fit the category presented in each question.

1.	Voiced consonants:	Л	Н	Ш	Ж	Й
2.	Voiceless consonants:	Л	Н	Ш	Ж	Й
3.	Hard-series vowels:	Э	Е			
4.	Soft-series vowels:	Э	Е			

Considering each combination of letters below, underline the …

5.	Hard consonants:	Нет Жест Шей Леш Тел Сжал Рай
6.	Soft consonants:	Нет Жест Шей Леш Тел Сжал Рай

Lesson 6

You've learned to recognize and pronounce seven new Russian letters in Lesson 5 including two vowel letters (Ээ Ее) and five consonant letters (Лл, Нн, Шш, Жж, Йй) in both romanface and Italics. Now you'll learn how to recognize and read those same letters when written in Russian cursive script. At the end of this lesson, you will know 21 of the 33 letters of the Russian alphabet in both print and cursive scripts.

Review

6.1   Review

Write out these letter combinations to review how they are written in cursive. **You can hear the sounds of these letter combinations in audio file 6.1.**

6.1-1   бюр   _____   _____

6.1-2   Кум   _____   _____

6.1-3   губ   _____   _____

6.1-4   бюг   _____   _____

6.1-5   мяб   _____   _____

6.1-6   гук   _____   _____

6.1-7   бюс   _____   _____

6.1-8   дуб   _____   _____

6.1-9   Паз   _____   _____

6.1-10 Бас   _____   _____

New Letters

6.2   Лл *Лл*

Like the Russian letters Яя and Мм, Russian Лл also requires a little hook in its bottom left "corner." This little hook in the bottom left corner distinguishes Лл from Пп. Start writing the letter Лл from this hook. Practice these combinations:

6.2-0a Л   _____   _____

6.2-0b л   _____   _____

6.2-1   Ляп   _____   _____

6.2-2   Ляз   _____   _____

6.2-3 бал _____ _____

6.2-4 мял _____ _____

6.3 Жж *Жж*

This letter connects to the letters which precede it at the top left corner; it connects to the letters which follow it on the bottom right. Look for this letter as a symbol on the door for the women's room in Russian-speaking countries. Practice these combinations:

6.3-0a Ж _____ _____

6.3-0b ж _____ _____

6.3-1 Жук _____ _____

6.3-2 Жаб _____ _____

6.3-3 паж _____ _____

6.3-4 пуж _____ _____

      Стаж _____ _____

      краж _____ _____

      сжал _____ _____

      Зжат _____ _____

6.4 Шш *Шш*

This letter has a flat bottom, unlike the English letter that may bear some resemblance to it. Also, remember to connect to the letter that follows it by connecting from the bottom right. Practice these combinations:

6.4-0a Ш _____ _____

6.4-0b ш _____ _____

6.4-1 Шаг _____ _____

6.4-2 шат _____ _____

6.4-3 баш _____ _____

      Муш _____ _____

таш _____ _____

Сташ _____ _____

Праш _____ _____

6.5   Нн *Нн*

Connect to the letters that follow this one from the bottom right. Practice these combinations:

6.5-0a   Н _____ _____

6.5-0b   н _____ _____

6.5-1   Нап _____ _____

6.5-2   Нюм _____ _____

6.5-3   анк _____ _____

Шанс _____ _____

6.5-5   нал _____ _____

Жант _____ _____

ранг _____ _____

6.6   Йй *Йй*

The upper case form of this letter is rarely used: it occurs **only** in foreign borrowings spelled out in Russian letters. The semi-circle above the letter is obligatory. Practice these combinations:

6.6-0a   Й _____ _____

6.6-0b   й _____ _____

6.6-1   май _____ _____

6.6-2   Дай _____ _____

6.6-3   Жуй _____ _____

6.6-4   Лей _____ _____

6.6-5   Буй _____ _____

6.6-6   Зяй _____ _____

Рай _____ _____

6.7   Ээ *Ээ*

Connect to the letters that follow this one from the middle stroke. Be sure to distinguish this letter from the consonant Зз. Practice these combinations:

6.7-0a   Э   _____   _____

6.7-0b   э   _____   _____

6.7-1   Эл   _____   _____

6.7-2   Эс   _____   _____

       Эм   _____   _____

       Эр   _____   _____

6.7-5   Бэ   _____   _____

6.7-6   Зэ   _____   _____

       эл   _____   _____

       эс   _____   _____

6.7-9   эм   _____   _____

6.7-10   эр   _____   _____

6.8   Ее *Ее*

This Russian letter is written in a way that is very similar to English Ee. Practice these combinations:

6.8-0a   Е   _____   _____

6.8-0b   е   _____   _____

6.8-1   Ем   _____   _____

6.8-2   Еш   _____   _____

6.8-3   Еж   _____   _____

6.8-4   Ел   _____   _____

6.8-5   Зел   _____   _____

6.8-6   Зек   _____   _____

Summary Practice

6.9   Practice I: writing with audio files. Practice writing out these letter combinations; check the audio files to monitor your pronunciation. Letter combinations marked with an asterisk are accompanied by video files 6.9-1, 6.9-2, etc.:

1.   Жеб* _____   _____
2.   жап* _____   _____
3.   Шед* _____   _____
4.   жед* _____   _____
5.   жар* _____   _____
6.   шек* _____   _____
7.   шур* _____   _____
8.   жат* _____   _____
9.   Шеб* _____   _____
10.   Шей* _____   _____
11.   Зеш* _____   _____
12.   нет* _____   _____
13.   Жей* _____   _____
14.   тянк* _____   _____
15.   ей* _____   _____
16.   Эр
17.   жеш* _____   _____
18.   Лей* _____   _____
19.   Эс* _____   _____
20.   Ляп* _____   _____
21.   Жур* _____   _____
22.   ляк* _____   _____
23.   лям* _____   _____
24.   жас* _____   _____
25.   шас* _____   _____
26.   анк* _____   _____
27.   бал* _____   _____
28.   баш* _____   _____
29.   Дай* _____   _____
30.   май* _____   _____
31.   Даш _____   _____

32.	Еж*	_____	_____
33.	зек*	_____	_____
34.	Ней	_____	_____
35.	Жуй*	_____	_____
36.	Куй	_____	_____
37.	Тюй*	_____	_____
38.	жус*	_____	_____
39.	Шаж	_____	_____
40.	шат*	_____	_____

6.10   Practice II: Practice these letter combinations. The sound file is start6-10.mp3; the video files are 6.10-1, 6.10-2, etc.

1.	Дэ*	_____	_____
2.	дер*	_____	_____
3.	эн*	_____	_____
4.	Гай*	_____	_____
5.	Гуй*	_____	_____
6.	луж*	_____	_____
7.	лет*	_____	_____
8.	Люд*	_____	_____
9.	Мяй*	_____	_____
10.	Наб*	_____	_____
11.	беш*	_____	_____
12.	санг*	_____	_____
13.	шар*	_____	_____
14.	шест*	_____	_____
15.	шезд*	_____	_____
16.	сей*	_____	_____
17.	сеш*	_____	_____
18.	Тэ*	_____	_____
19.	ест*	_____	_____
20.	жук*	_____	_____

Dictation

6.11   Listen to the tape and write out the sounds you hear in Cyrillic cursive letters. If it is possible to write the same sound combination in more than one different way, due to rules governing voiced and voiceless consonants, the sound will recur in two successive dictation items. In that case, be sure to write it out in two different spellings. There are 20 items in the dictation.

Lesson 7

You have learned 21 of the 33 letters of the Cyrillic alphabet in Lessons 1-6. These 21 letters include 6 vowels and 15 consonants:

Hard-Series Vowels	А	У	Э						
Soft-Series Vowels	Я	Ю	Е						

Voiced Consonants	З	Д	Б	Г	Ж	Р	М	Л	Н	Й
Voiceless Consonants	С	Т	П	К	Ш					

All but three of the consonants you've learned so far can be hard or soft, although due to the spelling rules, four of the consonant letters (Гг, Кк, Шш, Жж) that cannot be followed by soft-series vowels Яя, Юю have thus far appeared only in contexts in which they are hard. Two of the consonants you've learned so far (Шш, Жж) are group 1 consonants that are always hard; one consonant (Йй), of those you've learned so far, is a "group 2 consonant" (consonants that are always soft).

In this lesson you will learn 6 more letters, of which two will be vowel letters and four - consonant letters. Before we go forward, let's review.

Review

Remember, there are three groups of consonant letters in Russian:

1) consonants that are <u>always hard</u> (including Шш, Жж and one more letter presented in this lesson)
2) consonants that are <u>always soft</u> (including Йй and two more consonants to be presented in lesson 9)
3) consonants that may be <u>either hard or soft</u>, depending on the phonetic context (Тт, Сс, Рр, Дд, Зз, Пп, Кк, Мм, Бб, Гг, Лл, Нн)

Consonants of group 3 are hard if:

- Followed by another hard consonant or a hard-series vowel (Аа, Уу, Ээ)
- Word-final
- Followed by the hard-sign (see Lesson 9)

Consonants of group 3 are soft if:

- Followed by another soft consonant or a soft-series vowel (Яя, Юю, Ее)
- Followed by the soft-sign (see Lesson 9).

7.1   Hard and Soft Consonants

In each pair of sound combinations below, the first pair features a **hard** word-initial consonant, while the second pair features a **soft** word initial consonant. Each pair of sound combinations, in a given row, represents a significant contrast in the word-initial consonant: hard vs. soft.

Тус   Тюс

Маш   *Мяш*

Жен   Сен

Шез   *Нез*

Пэ   Пей

Бал   *Бял*

7.2   Each pair of sound combinations in the same row below is **pronounced identically, even though they are spelled differently**. Remember that voiced consonants in word-final position are pronounced as if they were their voiceless mate.

Сташ   Стаж

Рят   *Ряд*

Зуп   *Зуб*

Лес   Лез

Нош   *Нож*

Нож

7.3   When the voiceless consonant is followed by a voiced consonant, remember that it is pronounced like its voiced mate . (Exception: this pattern does not hold for the following letter combinations: СМ, СН, СЛ) The sounds below in the same row are **pronounced the same, even though they are spelled differently**.

Сдер   Здер

Сдре   Здре

Сдрес   Здрес

Сдряс   *Здряс*

Сгер   *Згер*

Сгум   *Згум*

Сгрек   Згрек

Сгрюм   Згрюм

New Letters

In this lesson you will learn 6 new letters, of which 2 are vowel letters and 4 are consonant letters. They will be presented in a sequence that makes pedagogical sense, but is not the same as alphabetical order. The letters are presented below, underscored in the Russian alphabet presented in alphabetical order.

Аа Бб <u>Вв</u> Гг Дд Ее <u>Ёё</u> Жж Зз Ии Йй Кк Лл Мм Нн <u>Оо</u> Пп Рр Сс Тт Уу <u>Фф</u> <u>Хх</u> <u>Цц</u> Чч Шш Щщ Ъъ Ыы Ьь Ээ Юю Яя

7.4   Хх *Хх*

Russian Хх is a voiceless consonant (without a voiced mate) that may be pronounced hard or soft, depending on the phonetic context in which it finds itself.   Listen to these sounds, distinguishing between hard and soft Хх *Хх*. To pronounce hard Хх, move the back of your tongue toward the back of your mouth and let it form a barrier to the flow of air. To pronounce soft Хх, move the midsection of your tongue towards the soft palate of your mouth.

Hard Хх *Хх*	**Soft Хх *Хх***
Хат	Хет
Хан	Хен

7.5   Хх and Spelling Rules

Never write Яя or Юю after Хх. Write Аа or Уу instead. (This letter is in the same group as the hushers with regards to this spelling rule.) For now the only way to have soft Хх is with Ее, as shown in section 7.4.

7.6   More practice with Хх

Practice these sound combinations.

Ах	Ха
Хай	*Ях*
Сах	Тах
Эх	*Хам*
Гах	Ух
Мах	*Бах*
Хей	Хек
Тюх	*Рюх*
Шах	Жах

Бах

7.7   Цц *Цц*

The letter Цц *Цц* is a voiceless consonant (no voiced mate) that is always hard. Together with
Шш, Жж, it completes the group of consonants that is always hard. Like Шш, Жж, when Цц is
followed by soft-series vowel Ее, the pronunciation sounds like Цэ. To pronounce this sound,
place the tip of your tongue against the hard palate and then, as the air is flowing out of your
mouth, move the tip of the tongue against the inner surface of your upper front teeth. Practice
with these combinations:

Цат	Цет
Цап	*Цеп*
Цак	Цек
Цан	*Цен*
Бац	Рац
Мац	*Мяц*
Цум	Цех
Жей	*Цей*
Цент	Плац

7.8   Spelling Rules

Just as with Шш, Жж, the vowels Яя, Ю,ю can not be written after Цц. Use Аа, Уу instead.

7.9   Special ending – тся

Some common Russian verbs end with the letters - тся. When these letters are at the end of a
verb, they are pronounced like"tsuh" in the English phrase "it's something." (File this bit of
information away for later!)

7.10   Фф *Фф*

The Russian consonant Фф *Фф* is a voiceless consonant (with a voiced mate to be presented
shortly) that may be hard or soft. This letter is somewhat infrequent in Russian because it
entered the alphabet relatively late in the history of the Russian language. Listen and practice
with these examples:

Фас	Фяс
Фаз	*Фяз*
Фут	Фют
Фуд	*Фюд*
Фэш	Феш
Фэж	*Феж*
Паф	Пяф
Уф	*Юф*
Эф	Еф

7.11   Вв *Вв*

The Russian consonant Вв is a voiced consonant, the mate of Фф, that can be pronounced either hard or soft. Note that the italic lower-case *в* looks like the cursive form of the English lower-case letter "b". Be careful to distinguish Бб / Вв! Practice with these sounds:

Ваш	Баш
Сав	*Саб*
Бяц	Вяц
Рев	*Реб*
Бес	Вес
Бах	*Вах*
Шув	Шуб
Бец	*Вец*
Вяр	Бяр
Бух	*Вух*

7.12   Voiced / Voiceless Вв Фф

Sounds in the same row are pronounced identically, even though they are spelled differently.

Шеф	*Шев*
Пуф	Пув
Зеф	*Зев*
Лаф	Лав
Мяф	*Мяв*
Пюф	Пюв
Жуф	*Жув*
Эф	Эв

7.13   Оо *Оо*

The Russian vowel Оо is a hard-series vowel. To pronounce it, be sure to keep your lips rounded throughout the utterance of the sound. It must never sound like the closed English sound typical of the "surfer" accent in "totally," but should sound more like the New York accent in "dawn" or the British accent in "born." It never has a y-glide. Practice with these examples:

Он	Ош
Ос	*От*
Оф	Оз

Ол   *Ор*

Вон   *Ров*

Ок   Ош

Сок   нос

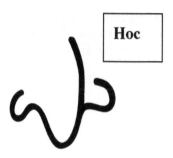

Нос

7.14   Spelling Rules and Оо

Spelling rules require that after Шш, Жж, Цц, one can never write *unstressed* Оо. (You'll learn more about stressed vowels in Lesson 11.) Write Ее instead.

But Гг, Кк, Хх + Оо = О-кей! (okay)

7.15   More practice with Оо

Practice with these sound combinations:

Дом   Вой

Зох   *Воц*

Вош   Ой

Ош   *Он*

Жолт   Шол   (assume the vowel is stressed!)

Ом   *Ост*

Дом

7.16   Combination: Св

For the sound combinations Сл, Св, См, Сн, Ср there is no "voicing" of the voiceless initial consonant in the cluster. Practice with these sound combinations:

Свал   Звал

Снег   *Знег*

Сруб   Зруб

Смак	*Змак*
Слон	Злон
Свой	*Звой*
Смол	Змол

СЛОН

7.17 Ёё *Ёё*

The last letter to be presented in this lesson is the soft-series vowel Ёё. In printed materials for learners of Russian, the two dots above the character are usually included (printed). In materials printed for native speakers of Russian, the two dots are generally omitted. Russians know that the two dots are there because they must be there from the context. For the time being, you should always write the two dots and you can look for them in the printed materials you are given (including your textbook.) Later in your learning career, as you look at authentic materials from Russia, you will get used to figuring out when the two dots are "implied" even when they are not printed. Practice these sound combinations:

Зон	Зён
Ров	*Рёв*
Нос	Нёс
Сток	*Стёк*
Вон	Вён
Лош	*Лёш*
Лог	Лёг
Сок	*Сёк*
Бор	Бёр
Флор	*Флёр*
Мост	Мёст
Стоп	*Стён*
Полк	Пёлк

Мост

7.18   Ёё Ёё in word-initial position

This vowel letter has a y-glide (like Яя, Юю). Practice it in the combinations below:

Он	ён
Ос	*ёс*
Ок	ёк
Ож	*ёж*

ёж

7.19   Ёё and Hard Consonants

When soft-series vowel Ёё follows a group 1 consonant (Шш, Жж, Цц), that consonant is still pronounced hard, just as if it were followed by the hard-series vowel Оо. The sounds in each row are pronounced identically, even though they are spelled differently: (assume all vowels below are stressed!)

Жолт	Жёлт
Жолд	*Жёлд*
Шолк	Шёлк
Шолг	*Шёлг*
Цос	Цёс
Цоз	*Цёз*

Summary Practice

7.20   Practice these sounds as a review for all the sounds and letters of Lessons 1-7. Remember that voiced consonants in word-final position are pronounced like their voiceless mates (except for those voiced consonants that are "mateless").

1. Цан	23. Баж	46. Вош	69. Стёк
2. Цах	24. Бац	47. Вёш	70. Сдёк
3. Цам	25. Вай	48. Он	71. Сков
4. Цак	26. Вух	49. Ор	72. Сгов
5. Мац	27. Вец	50. Ос	73. Жёлт
6. Спец	28. Вез	51. От	74. Шёлк
7. Жец	29. Вег	52. Ов	75. Шёл
8. Цен	30. Бег	53. Ок	76. Воз
9. Цей	31. Бац	54. Ён	77. Вёз
10. Цел	32. Бай	55. Ёр	78. Старт
11. Цех	33. Бух	56. Ёс	79. Сдарт
12. Ваш	34. Бец	57. Ёт	80. Сдеш
13. Вяр	35. Без	58. Ёв	81. Здеш
14. Вах	36. Вой	59. Ах	82. Свал
15. Вес	37. Вёй	60. Ха	83. Звал
16. Век	38. Зох	61. Ох	84. Срок
17. Важ	39. Зёх	62. Эх	85. Зрок
18. Баш	40. Сок	63. Ух	86. Сруб
19. Бяр	41. Сёк	64. Хей	87. Зруб
20. Бах	42. Нос	65. Сав	88. Слон
21. Бес	43. Нёс	66. Саф	89. Злон
22. Бек	44. Дом	67. Пуф	90. Смол
	45. Дём	68. Пув	

Self-Quiz

Part 1. Listen to the sounds in the sound file and circle the letter combination that best represents the spelling of that sound.

1	Шок	Жок	Шёг
2	Вех	Бег	Бех
3	Цаб	Шап	Жап
4	Вон	Вён	Фён
5	Вай	Вей	Бей
6	Шей	Цей	Жей
7	Пав	Лав	Поф
8	Шех	Цех	Цеф
9	Фан	Цан	Хан
10	Роб	Лоб	Доб
11	Вжам	Вшам	Фам
12	Сдой	Стой	Здёй
13	Ёп	Яп	Оп
14	Эв	Ев	Яв
15	Лэй	Лей	Лай
16	Вей	Бэй	Бей
17	Жей	Цей	Шей
18	Цех	Цеш	Шех
19	Свой	Звой	Сбой
20	Соф	Зов	Зёв

Part 2. Circle the letters that best fit the category presented in each question.

1.	Voiced consonants:	Х	Ц	Ф	В
2.	Voiceless consonants:	Х	Ц	Ф	В
3.	Hard-series vowels:	О	Ё		
4.	Soft-series vowels:	О	Ё		

Considering each combination of letters below, underline the …

5.	Hard consonants:	Снег	Нёс	Шёл	Вох	Фюм	Цап
6.	Soft consonants:	Снег	Нёс	Шёл	Вох	Фюм	Цап

Lesson 8

You've learned to recognize and pronounce six new Russian letters in Lesson 7 including two vowel letters (Оо Ёё) and four consonant letters (Хх, Цц, Фф, Вв) in both romanface and Italics. Now you'll learn how to recognize and read those same letters when written in Russian cursive script. At the end of this lesson, you will know 27 of the 33 letters of the Russian alphabet in both print and cursive scripts.

Review

8.1   Review

Write out these letter combinations to review how they are written in cursive.

8.1-1	жат	_____	_____
8.1-2	Шеб	_____	_____
	Танк	_____	_____
8.1-4	Лей	_____	_____
	Шал	_____	_____
8.1-6	эр	_____	_____
8.1-7	Тэ	_____	_____
8.1-8	Нет	_____	_____
8.1-9	Жур	_____	_____
8.1-10	Бал	_____	_____
	бяш	_____	_____
	Люк	_____	_____
8.1-13	Дай	_____	_____
8.1-14	Еш	_____	_____
8.1-15	Ёж	_____	_____

New Letters

8.2   Фф *Фф*

Practice this letter step by step. Practice these combinations:

8.2-0a Ф   _____ _____

8.2-0b ф   _____ _____

8.2-1   Фяс   _____   _____

8.2-2   Фюм   _____   _____

8.2-3   фас   _____   _____

8.2-4   Фум   _____   _____

8.2-5   паф   _____   _____

        шаф   _____   _____

8.3   Вв *Вв*

This letter is written just like the English letter it resembles, but of course the two letters are pronounced differently, so be sure to distinguish them. Practice these combinations:

8.3-0a В   _____   _____

8.3-0b в   _____   _____

8.3-1   Ваш   _____   _____

8.3-2   Вес   _____   _____

        Сев   _____   _____

        Лев   _____   _____

        Плов   _____   _____

        Яв   _____   _____

8.4   Цц *Цц*

This letter must have a little tail at the bottom right. Practice these combinations:

8.4-0a Ц   _____   _____

8.4-0b ц   _____   _____

8.4-1   Цап   _____   _____

8.4-2   Цум   _____   _____

8.4-3   бац   _____   _____

8.4-4 Цан _____ _____

8.4-5 спец _____ _____

8.5 Хх *Хх*

This letter connects to letters that follow it from the **<u>bottom right</u>**. Practice these combinations:

8.5-0a X _____ _____

8.5-0b x _____ _____

8.5-1 Хан _____ _____

8.5-2 Хам _____ _____

     хан _____ _____

8.5-4 хам _____ _____

8.5-5 Хей _____ _____

8.5-6 Сах _____ _____

     Тех _____ _____

8.6 Оо *Оо*, Ёё *Ёё*

These letters are written just like the English letters (except you must add the two dots for the Ёё) Practice these combinations:

8.6-0a O _____ _____

8.6-0b o _____ _____

8.6-0c Ё _____ _____

8.6-0d ё _____ _____

8.6-1 Ой _____ _____

     Ёй _____ _____

8.6-3 вош _____ _____

8.6-4 Ёж _____ _____

     Шёлк _____ _____

Полк   _____   _____

Summary Practice

8.7   Practice I with audio files: Practice writing out these letter combinations. Letter combinations marked with an asterisk have a corresponding video file (8.7-1, 8.7-2, etc.) The pronunciation of all the letter combinations in this section may be checked in the audio file start8-7.mp3

1.   Уф*   _____   _____
2.   жаф*   _____   _____
3.   Фаш   _____   _____
4.   век*   _____   _____
5.   бек*   _____   _____
6.   ров*   _____   _____
7.   Роб   _____   _____
8.   цей*   _____   _____
9.   спец*   _____   _____
10.   Шолт   _____   _____
11.   шеф*   _____   _____
12.   Цум*   _____   _____
13.   ах*   _____   _____
14.   Ох   _____   _____
15.   эх*   _____   _____
16.   Вес*   _____   _____
17.   Фум*   _____   _____
18.   Эф*   _____   _____
19.   сах*   _____   _____
20.   Тех   _____   _____
21.   бац*   _____   _____
22.   Хей   _____   _____
23.   ой*   _____   _____
24.   эй   _____   _____
25.   эх*   _____   _____
26.   цел*   _____   _____
27.   гах*   _____   _____

28.	Бах	_____	_____
29.	Вай	_____	_____
30.	нёс*	_____	_____
31.	Стоп	_____	_____
32.	Стёк	_____	_____
33.	Вез	_____	_____
34.	Вёз	_____	_____
35.	без	_____	_____
36.	бёз	_____	_____
37.	блюз	_____	_____
38.	слон	_____	_____
39.	сок*	_____	_____
40.	шок	_____	_____

8.8   Practice II. Practice these letter combinations. The sound file is start8-8.mp3; the video files are 8.8-1, 8.8-2, etc.

1.	баш*	_____	_____
2.	баж*	_____	_____
3.	цех*	_____	_____
4.	Цул *	_____	_____
5.	Фэ *	_____	_____
6.	Фет*	_____	_____
7.	фюм*	_____	_____
8.	лоф*	_____	_____
9.	лёв*	_____	_____
10.	пуф*	_____	_____
11.	рёв*	_____	_____
12.	шол*	_____	_____
13.	шолк*	_____	_____
14.	свой*	_____	_____
15.	ух*	_____	_____
16.	Вой*	_____	_____
17.	вер*	_____	_____
18.	Вёй*	_____	_____
19.	Ляб*	_____	_____
20.	Ёш*	_____	_____

21. жолт* _____   _____

22. звёзд* _____   _____

23. зборт* _____   _____

24. шанк* _____   _____

25. ха-ха-ха*   _____

                                      _____

Dictation

8.9   Listen to the tape and write out the sounds you hear in Cyrillic cursive letters. If it is possible to write the same sound combination in more than one different way, due to rules governing voiced and voiceless consonants, the sound will recur in two successive dictation items. In that case, be sure to write it out in two different spellings. There are 20 items in this dictation

Lesson 9

You have learned 27 of the 33 letters of the Cyrillic alphabet in Lessons 1-8. These 27 letters include 8 vowels and 25 consonants:

Hard-Series Vowels	А	У	Э	О	
Soft-Series Vowels	Я	Ю	Е	Ё	
Paired Voiced Consonants	З	Д	Б	Г	Ж	В
Paired Voiceless Consonants	С	Т	П	К	Ш	Ф
Unpaired Voiced Consonants	Р	М	Л	Н	Й	
Unpaired Voiceless Consonants	Х	Ц				

All but four of the consonants you've learned so far can be hard or soft, although due to the spelling rules, four of the consonant letters (Гг, Кк, Шш, Жж) that cannot be followed by soft-series vowels Яя, Юю have thus far appeared only in contexts in which they are hard. Three of the consonants you've learned so far (Шш, Жж, Цц) are "group 1 consonants" (always hard); one consonant (Йй), of those you've learned so far, is a "group 2 consonant" (always soft). You'll learn two more group 2 consonants in this lesson.

Speaking of which, in this lesson you'll learn the remaining 6 letters of the Russian alphabet. Two of these are vowel letters, two are consonant letters, and two are something else entirely! (Read on to learn more!) But first, let's review.

Review

9.1   Hard and Soft Consonants

Remember, there are three groups of consonant letters in Russian:

1) consonants that are <u>always hard</u> (Шш, Жж, Цц)

2) consonants that are <u>always soft</u> (Йй and two more consonants to be presented in this lesson)

3) consonants that may be <u>either hard or soft</u>, depending on the phonetic context (Тт, Сс, Рр, Дд, Зз, Пп, Кк, Мм, Бб, Гг, Лл, Нн, Хх, Фф, Вв)

Consonants of group 3 are hard if:

- Followed by another hard consonant or a hard-series vowel (Аа, Уу, Ээ, Оо)
- Word-final
- Followed by the hard-sign (see later in this lesson)

Consonants of group 3 are soft if:

- Followed by another soft consonant or a soft-series vowel (Яя, Юю, Ее, Ёё)
- Followed by the soft-sign (see later in this lesson).

In each pair of sound combinations below, the first pair features a **hard** word-initial consonant, while the second pair features a **soft** word initial consonant.

Each pair of sound combinations, in a given row, represents a significant contrast in the word-initial consonant: hard vs. soft.

Сок	Сёк
Вал	*Вял*
Фум	Фюм
Цех	*Тех*
Шам	Сям
Жев	*Лев*
Май	Мяй
Нос	*Нёс*
Дул	Дюл

Лев

9.2   Each pair of sound combinations in the same row below is **pronounced identically, even though they are spelled differently.** Remember that voiced consonants in word-final position are pronounced as if they were their voiceless mate.

Зоф	Зов
Паш	*Паж*
Ряп	Ряб
Гус	*Гуз*
Лёт	Лёд
Юк	*Юг*

9.3   When the voiceless consonant is followed by a voiced consonant, remember that it is pronounced like its voiced mate . (Exception: this pattern does not hold for the following letter combinations: СМ, СН, СЛ, СВ) The sounds below in the same row are **pronounced the same, even though they are spelled differently**.

Сдре	*Здре*
Сдер	Здер
Сгрек	*Згрек*
Сгрюм	Згрюм
Сдрес	*Здрес*
Сгер	Згер
Сдряс	*Здряс*
Сгум	Згум

New Letters

In this lesson you will learn 6 new letters, of which 2 are vowel letters, 2 –consonant letters and 2 – something else entirely. They will be presented in a sequence that makes pedagogical sense, but is not the same as alphabetical order. The letters are presented below, underscored in the Russian alphabet presented in alphabetical order.

Аа Бб Вв Гг Дд Ее Ёё Жж Зз <u>Ии</u> Йй Кк Лл Мм Нн Оо Пп
Рр Сс Тт Уу Фф Хх Цц <u>Чч</u> Шш <u>Щщ</u> <u>Ъъ</u> <u>Ыы</u> <u>Ьь</u> Ээ Юю Яя

9.4   Щщ *Щщ*

Russian Щщ is a voiceless consonant (without a voiced mate) that is always soft. It is another husher. To pronounce it, have the tip of your tongue touch the floor of your mouth just behind your lower teeth. Arch the middle of your tongue towards the soft palate of your mouth and obstruct the air flowing through your mouth with the middle of your tongue just barely touching your soft palate. Compare the sound you make when holding this position, with the sound you make for Шш , for which you are pointing the tip of your tongue towards the hard palate of your mouth (back part of the roof of your mouth). Practice distinguishing between these pairs of sounds:

Hard Husher	**Soft Husher**
Шан	Щан
Шел	*Щел*
Шум	Щум
Шар	*Щар*
Шок	Щок

Шав	*Щав*
Шас	Щас
Шет	*Щет*
Шур	Щур
Вош	*Вощ*
Таш	Тащ
Реш	*Рещ*
Стяш	Стящ
Мюш	*Мющ*

9.5   Щщ + Ее / Ее + Щщ

Since Щщ is a group 2 consonant (always soft), we can add to our list of examples for the pronunciation of Ее as demonstrated in the next two subsections, 9.5.1 and 9.5.2

9.5.1   Hard Consonant + E + Soft Consonant

Жещ

Цещ

Шей

9.5.2   Soft Consonant + E + Soft Consonant

Мещ

Зещ

Лей

9.6   Щщ + Оо / Ёё

Since Щщ is a husher, like Шш, Жж, unstressed Оо cannot be written after Щщ. Moreover, there is no difference in pronunciation between Що/Щё or Ще/Щэ:

Щёк	*Щок*
Щет	Щэт
Шён	*Шон*
Шет	Шэт
Жёл	*Жол*
Жеп	Жэп

9.7   More practice with Щщ

Щуб

Рещ

Вощ

Щад

Щав

Жещ

Цещ

Сащ

Щёг

Мещ

Щён

Пещ

Щел

9.8   Practice distinguishing Щщ/Шш

Ща	Ша
Щу	*Шу*
Ще	Ше
Що	*Шо*
Щар	Шар
Щум	*Шум*
Щеп	Шеб
Щок	*Шок*

9.9   Чч *Чч*

The Russian consonant Чч is a voiceless consonant (without a voiced mate) that is always soft. It is the third and final group 2 consonant (together with Йй Щщ): these three Russian consonants are the consonants that are always soft. To pronounce this sound, let the midsection of your tongue lightly touch the soft palate and then gradually move it forward as the air flows past your teeth. Practice with these sounds:

Чар	Чур
Чей	*Чай*
Чай	Чу
Чем	*Чек*
Чук	Чоп

Чай

9.10   Чч + Ее / Ее + Чч

Since Чч is a group 2 consonant (always soft), we can add to our list of examples for the pronunciation of Ее:

9.10.1   Hard Consonant + E + Soft Consonant

Шей

Жещ

Цеч

9.10.2   Soft Consonant + E + Soft Consonant

Мещ

Печ

Тей

9.11   The Last Husher and Spelling Rules

This letter is the last of the four hushers in Russian (Шш, Жж, Щщ, Чч) and it is governed by the same rules as the other hushers. After Чч you cannot write unstressed О, but there is no difference in pronunciation between чо / чё. After Чч you cannot write Яя, Юю; always write Аа, Уу instead.

9.12   С + ч

When the letter Чч is preceded by Сс, the two letters are pronounced like Щщ. Practice with these sound combinations: sounds in the same row are pronounced identically, even though they are spelled differently.

Счас	Щас	Щаз
Счей	*Щей*	
Счёт	Щёт	Щёд
Счем	*Щем*	
Счук	Щук	Щуг

9.13   Ыы *Ыы*

The Russian hard-series vowel Ыы is never written in word-initial position in a genuine Russian word. It may occur in word-initial position for a foreign borrowing into Russian (but that, too, is rare.) To pronounce this sound, smile as if to pronounce the English sound "ee" (as in "deed") but try to say "oo" (as in "dude") without moving your lips. Listen and practice with these examples:

Мы	*we*
Ты	*you (singular and informal)*
Вы	*you (plural or formal)*
Сын	*son*
Бык	*bull (the animal)*

Бык

Рыл	*poked around (past tense verb form)*
Тыл	*home front*
Был	*was (past tense verb form)*
Выл	*howled (past tense verb form)*
Сыр	*cheese*
Сыт	*satisfied, sated*
Мыт	*washed*

Сыр

9.14   Spelling Rules and Ыы

The spelling rules of Russian dictate that the vowel letter Ыы may never be written after any of the following letters: Г, К, Х, Ш, Ж, Щ, Ч. After these letters, you have to write another vowel letter, which is introduced in section 9.15. Note that the combination Цы is allowed. (In lesson 11 you'll learn some names of famous Russians that have this combination of letters.)

9.15   Ии *Ии*

The vowel letter Ии is a soft-series vowel that, unlike the other soft-series vowels (Яя, Юю, Ее, Ёё) has no y-glide. Listen and compare this vowel sound with the vowel sound Ыы.

Мыт	Мит
Сын	*Син*
Лып	Лип
Бык	*Бик*
Мы	Ми
Ты	*Ти*
Был	Бил
Тыл	*Тил*
Тык	Тик
Выл	*Вил*
Рым	Рим

Сын

9.16   Word-initial Ии *Ии*

As noted earlier, Ии has no y-glide. In fact, when it is in word-initial position and the preceding word ends in a hard consonant, Ии is pronounced as if it were, in fact, Ыы. In the examples in this section, imagine that the preceding words end in a consonant.

Н	ит
Л	*ис*
Р	ик
С	*им*
Ф	ир

9.17   Spelling Rules and Ии / Ыы

Remember, the spelling rules say that you cannot write Ыы after any of the following letters: Кк, Гг, Хх, Щщ, Шш, Щщ, Чч. Instead, write Ии. However, after the "hard" hushers Шш, Жж, we write Ии, but pronounce Ыы, as shown in the examples below. Remember, to pronounce the hard hushers you have to point the tip of your tongue towards your hard upper palate. If you do this correctly, you will automatically pronounce the vowel sound that follows correctly, as well.

(Audio file 9.17 begins here.)

Жир

Шир

Жил

Шил

Шит

Жик

Шик

9.18   Combinations Чи, Щи

Compare the pronunctiation of soft and hard hushers with the vowel Ии:

Шир	Щир
Жир	*Чир*
Ши	Щи
Жин	*Чин*
Шип	Чип
Шик	*Щик*
Жил	Чил
Шил	*Щил*

Щи

9.19   Practice with Ии / Ыы

Син	*Сын*
Бик	Бык
Щин	*Шит*
Чин	Жин
Ми	*Мы*
Ви	Вы
Бил	*Был*
Тил	Тыл
Щил	*Шил*
Чил	Жил

9.20   Introducing the Soft Sign Ьь

Now you have learned 31 of the 33 letters of the Russian alphabet. There are only two more letters to learn and they are neither consonants nor vowels. These two letters are called the hard and soft signs, respectively. Think for a moment of these two English words: mad / made. What is the difference between these two words? What is the pronunciation of the "e" in "made"? It's usually called "silent e" in reading textbooks for schoolchildren in English-speaking countries. Silent "e" has no pronunciation of its own, but it affects the pronunciation of a letter or letters that precede it. Usually silent "e" only affects the preceding vowel (turning it from "short" to "long"), but sometimes it affects consonants, as in the words bath / bathe. (The silent "e" turns the voiceless "th" into a voiced "th".) The hard sign and soft sign play a similar role in Russian: they affect the pronunciation of the consonant sound(s) that precede them (and sometimes the vowel sounds too.)

The soft sign "softens" the pronunciation of a group 3 consonant that precedes it. Practice with these pairs of sounds:

Ас	Ась
Мыт	*Мыть*
Ос	Ось
Ал	*Аль*
Ут	Уть
Ен	*Ень*
Яс	Ясь
Ют	*Ють*
От	Оть
Ар	*Арь*
Был	Быль

Ет	*Еть*
Ел	Ель
Ат	*Ать*
Сем	Семь
Здес	*Здесь*
Вес	Весь
Ден	*День*
Стол	Столь

9.21 Soft Sign and Ee: Hard Consonant + Ee + Soft Consonant

Since the soft sign "softens" any consonant that precedes it, we can add to our examples for pronunciation of Ee as follows –: Hard Consonant + Ee + Soft Consonant

Жей	
Цель	*goal, objective*
Шень	
Цепь	*chain*
Жеть	
Шерь	
Жечь	*to burn*

9.22 Soft Sign and Ee: Soft Consonant + Ee + Soft Consonant

Since the soft sign "softens" any consonant that precedes it, we can add to our examples for pronunciation of Ee as follows –: Soft Consonant + Ee + Soft Consonant

Сей	*that (archaic)*
Мель	
Тень	*shadow*
Весь	*all, entire*
Меч	*sword*
Тесть	*father-in-law (for a man only)*
Семь	*seven*

9.23   Soft Sign + Soft-Series Vowel

When the soft sign is between a consonant and one of the soft-series vowels with a y-glide (Яя, Юю, Ее, Ёё), the y-glide is pronounced. Compare the different pronunciation of each "column" of sounds below. (Sounds in the same column are analogous except for the initial consonant sound.)

Да	Дя	Дья
До	Дё	Дьё
Сэ	Се	Сье
Су	Сю	Сью
Ла	Ля	Лья
Лу	Лю	Лью

9.24   Husher + Soft Sign at the end of words

When the soft sign follows one of the four hushers (Ш, Ж, Щ, Ч) at the end of a word, it does not affect pronunciation but merely conveys some grammatical information. This is not important for you to know now, but in case you're curious:

A noun ending in any husher + soft sign = The noun is *feminine, e.g.* ночь (night).
A verb form ending in Шш + soft sign = The verb is in the *2nd person singular form, e.g.,* пьёшь (you are drinking, singular, familiar)

Since the soft sign doesn't affect the pronunciation of the hushers which precede it, the sounds in the same row below are identical, despite the fact that they are spelled differently:

Вещ	Вещь
Реч	Речь
Вош	Вошь
Лож	Ложь
Доч	Дочь

Дочь

The right hand column above consists of actual Russian words meaning: *a thing, a speech, a louse (insect), a lie, a daughter.*

Now you have only one more letter left to learn!

9.25   Hard Sign Ъъ

The hard sign is the most infrequently used letters of the Russian alphabet today. It is used to indicate that the preceding consonant remains hard despite the fact that a soft-series vowel follows the hard sign. The hard sign sets up a kind of "barrier" between the hard consonant and the soft-series vowel. Compare these sounds (some of them are all actual words):

Сем	Съем	not a word / *[I] will eat up*
Сел	Съел	*sat down / ate up*
Сест	Съест	not a word / *[s/he] will eat up*
Сеш	Съешь	not a word / *[you] will eat up*

You should have heard a y-glide in the pronunciation of the words in the right-hand column. If you didn't hear it, go back and listen again.

9.26   Historical Note

Before the language reforms adopted by the Communists shortly after the revolution of November 1917, all Russian words ending in a consonant had to be followed by a soft sign or a hard sign to indicate whether the consonant was hard or soft. The communists decreed that all words ending in consonants would be hard except for those ending in the soft sign or any of the 3 consonants of group 2 (always soft) – Йй, Щщ, Чч. This language reform meant that books would become shorter because lots of hard signs could now be omitted. Legend has it that the novel *War and Peace* became 21 pages shorter when it was published in the new orthography.

Summary Practice

9.27   Practice

Now that you have learned all 33 letters of the Cyrillic alphabet, it's time to practice and review.

Remember that voiced consonants in word-final position are pronounced like their voiceless mates (except for those voiced consonants that are "mateless").

1. Цан	16. чур	*32. уть*	48. ос
2. шар	17. счем	33. та	*49. ось*
3. щел	*18. счёт*	34. тя	50. тест
4. шит	19. счас	*35. тья*	51. тесть
5. чик	20. цеч	36. син	*52. шил*
6. щёт	*21. жеч*	*37. сын*	53. жил
7. мыт	22. вещь	38. шир	54. щил
8. мыть	23. сья	*39. жир*	*55. ен*
9. шув	*24. весь*	40. чир	56. ень
10. щув	25. язь	*41. щир*	*57. рёв*
11. рещ	26. яз	42. ты	58. ляк
12. реч	*27. цел*	43. ти	*59. лёг*
13. реш	28. цель	*44. сеш*	60. стаж
14. меч	*29. сем*	45. съешь	
15. чу	30. семь	*46. сем*	
	31. ут	47. съем	

Self-Quiz

Part 1. Listen to the sounds in the sound file and circle the letter combination that best represents the spelling of that sound.

1	Жип	Шир	Шип
2	чей	Шей	Щей
3	Шит	щит	Чит
4	Мик	Смык	Мык
5	Син	Цын	Сын
6	Бал	баль	Даль
7	Донь	Дон	Дань
8	Сип	Цып	сып
9	Сем	съем	Сен
10	жест	Шесть	Честь
11	Миш	Мыч	мышь
12	въял	Вял	Вяр
13	мыл	Мы	Ми
14	Ест	есь	Есть
15	Шир	жир	Чир
16	Шей	чей	Щей
17	Спек	Снег	сбег
18	Столь	Сдол	Сдоль
19	Свой	Звой	Ствой
20	Сень	Рен	Рень

Part 2. Circle the letters that best fit the category presented in each question.

1.	Voiced consonants:	Ч	Щ
2.	Voiceless consonants:	Ч	Щ
3.	Hard-series vowels:	Ы	И
4.	Soft-series vowels:	Ы	И

Considering each combination of letters below, underline the ...

5.	Hard consonants:	Съезд Речь Шаль Цель Съем Жир
6.	Soft consonants:	Съезд Речь Шаль Цель Съем Жир

Lesson 10

You've learned to recognize and pronounce six new Russian letters in Lesson 9 including two vowel letters (Ыы, Ии) and two consonant letters (Чч, Щщ), as well as the hard sign (ъ) and soft sign (ь) in both romanface and Italics. Now you'll learn how to recognize and read those same letters when written in Russian cursive script. At the end of this lesson, you will know the entire Russian alphabet in both print and cursive scripts.

Review

10.1   Review

Write out these letter combinations to review how they are written in cursive. Letter combinations marked with an asterisk are accompanied by video files (10.1-2, 10.1-3, etc.).

1.   Хав   _____   _____

2.   Цел*   _____   _____

3.   шеф*   _____   _____

4.   ров*   _____   _____

5.   рёв*   _____   _____

6.   Бой   _____   _____

7.   Жест   _____   _____

8.   Шей*   _____   _____

9.   Ной   _____   _____

10.   Краж   _____   _____

11.   Стой   _____   _____

12.   Сбег   _____   _____

13.   Лёг   _____   _____

14.   Мел   _____   _____

15.   Фюм*   _____   _____

16.   ряд*   _____   _____

17.   Старт*   _____   _____

18.   Нож   _____   _____

19.   Эс*   _____   _____

20.   Эл*   _____   _____

21.   Шум*   _____   _____

22.   Тут   _____   _____

23.   буш*   _____   _____

24.   Глуш   _____   _____

New Letters

10.2   Чч *Чч*

Note that the tail of this letter curves to the right (while the tail of upper-case У curves to the left). Practice these combinations:

10.2-0a   Ч   _____   _____

10.2-0b   ч   _____   _____

10.2-1   Чей   _____   _____

10.2-2   Чар   _____   _____

10.2-3   Чем   _____   _____

10.2-4   чу   _____   _____

10.2-5   меч   _____   _____

10.2-6   жеч   _____   _____

10.3   Щщ *Щщ*

Don't forget the little tail in the bottom right corner of this letter; this tail distinguishes Щ from Ш. In cursive, some Russians write a bar under Ш. The bar is NEVER written under Щ. Remember, if you have a tail (Щ), you can't go to a bar (Ш)! Practice these combinations:

10.3-0a   Щ   _____   _____

10.3-0b   щ   _____   _____

10.3-1   Щав   _____   _____

10.3-2   Щи   _____   _____

10.3-3   щад   _____   _____

10.3-4   рещ   _____   _____

10.3-5   щас   _____   _____

10.3-6   вощ   _____   _____

10.4   Ии *Ии*

Don't write a semi-circle above this letter! Practice these combinations:

10.4-0a   И   _____   _____

10.4-0b   и   _____   _____

10.4-1   тик   _____   _____

10.4-2   Мит   _____   _____

10.4-3   ли   _____   _____

            Ил   _____   _____

10.4-5   Ир   _____   _____

10.4-6   щи   _____   _____

10.5   ы *ы*

This letter has no upper-case form. Remember, it is NEVER written with a dot (as is English "i"). Practice these combinations:

10.5-0a   not applicable (no upper-case form of this letter)

10.5-0b   ы _____   _____

10.5-1   Мы   _____   _____

10.5-2   Ты   _____   _____

10.5-3   Вы   _____   _____

10.5-4   сыр   _____   _____

            Тыл   _____   _____

10.5-6   бык   _____   _____

10.6   ь *ь* (Мягкий знак - Soft Sign)

This letter has no upper-case form. Practice these combinations:

10.6-0a   not applicable (no upper-case form)

10.6-0b   ь _____   _____

10.6-1	Есь	_____	_____
	Семь	_____	_____
10.6-3	сесть	_____	_____
	Речь	_____	_____
10.6-5	вещь	_____	_____
10.6-6	цель	_____	_____
10.6-7	дья	_____	_____
	Мья	_____	_____

10.7   ъ ⱬ (Твёрдый знак – Hard Sign)

This letter has no upper-case form. Practice these combinations:

10.7-0a   not applicable (no upper case form)

10.7-0b   ъ _____   _____

10.7-1 съезд   _____ _____

10.7-2 съест   _____ _____

10.7-3 съем   _____ _____

Summary Practice

10.8   Practice I: writing with audio files. Practice writing out these letter combinations. Letter combinations marked with an asterisk have a corresponding video file (10.8-1, 10.8-2, etc.). All the letter combinations are pronounced in audio file start10-8.mp3.

1.	Чай*	_____	_____
2.	меч*	_____	_____
3.	сащ*	_____	_____
4.	Речь	_____	_____
5.	щель*	_____	_____
6.	Цель	_____	_____

7.   бил* _____   _____

8.   был* _____   _____

9.   Выл _____   _____

10.   Вил _____   _____

11.   Течь _____   _____

12.   ли* _____   _____

13.   Шит _____   _____

14.   Щит _____   _____

15.   шит* _____   _____

16.   щит* _____   _____

17.   Жир* _____   _____

18.   шил* _____   _____

19.   тишь _____   _____

20.   сыр* _____   _____

21.   рис _____   _____

22.   Эль* _____   _____

23.   Ань* _____   _____

24.   Мыт* _____   _____

25.   мыть* _____   _____

26.   весь _____   _____

27.   арь* _____   _____

28.   вешь _____   _____

29.   цель* _____   _____

30.   щи* _____   _____

31.   чик _____   _____

32.   чек _____   _____

33.   счёт _____   _____

34.   шур _____   _____

35.   щур _____   _____

36.   вощ _____   _____

37.   семь _____   _____

38.   съем _____   _____

39.   съезд _____   _____

40.   съест _____   _____

10.9   Practice II. Practice these letter combinations. The sound file is start10-9.mp3; the video files are 10.9-1, 10.9-2, etc.

1. Аль* _____   _____
2. ань* _____   _____
3. бюдж* _____   _____
4. чар* _____   _____
5. друг* _____   _____
6. Эль* _____   _____
7. кровь* _____   _____
8. лык* _____   _____
9. мир* _____   _____
10. ось* _____   _____
11. рой* _____   _____
12. шаг* _____   _____
13. Щу* _____   _____
14. шид* _____   _____
15. сын* _____   _____
16. тык* _____   _____
17. уть* _____   _____
18. ясь* _____   _____
19. ень* _____   _____
20. есь* _____   _____

Dictation

10.10 Listen to the tape and write out the sounds you hear in Cyrillic cursive letters. If it is possible to write the same sound combination in more than one different way, due to rules governing voiced and voiceless consonants, the sound will recur in two successive dictation items. In that case, be sure to write it out in two different spellings. There are 20 items in the dictation.

Lesson 11

11.1   Introduction to Lexical Stress

In the previous 10 lessons, you've learned how to pronounce combinations of Russian sounds that are only one syllable long. Some of these combinations have been actual words. But most Russian words, as you may have guessed, are more than one syllable long. In this lesson, you'll learn the rules that govern the pronunciation of vowels in multisyllabic Russian words. These same rules have an impact on English. Consider, for example, the letter "a" in the words "garage" and "garbage". The letter "a" occurs in each of these two words, but in each word the letter "a" conveys two different sounds. (The letter "e" is silent in both words, playing a role life the Russian soft sign in affecting the pronunciation of the consonant letter that precedes it.) The difference in the pronunciation of each "a" in these words is due to the lexical stress. In the first word, "garage", the stress falls on the second syllable. The first "a" in this word is pronounced like "uh" as in "luck", while the second "a" in this word is pronounced like "ah" as in "hot" (in American pronunciation, not British.) The pattern of pronunciation is reversed in the word "garbage" because the stress falls on the first syllable, not the second.

Russian, like English, has a system of "stress" which affects the pronunciation of words that are more than one syllable in length. For this reason, all the sounds you have practiced in lessons 1-10 have been monosyllabic (that is, they consisted of only one syllable each.) In lesson 11 you'll learn how to pronounce words that are more than one syllable in length.

The stress of a word falls on the vowel in the syllable which receives the "downbeat" during the pronunciation of that word. In English every word may have more than one stress and words of three or more syllables typically do have two or more stresses. For example, IMmiGRAtion has two stresses, although the second stress (on the third syllable) is the dominant stress because it has greater stress than the first syllable. Pronunciation of any English word depends on where the stress falls. Consider the words "execute" and "executive", for example. The difference in stress can distinguish words in both English and Russian. Consider the italicized words in the following two sentences:

Tina just moved: what is her *address* now?
I have to *address* this problem right away!

In Russian, you can see the same phenomenon in pairs of words that are spelled identically but pronounced differently due to the difference in stress. Consider these words:

З<u>а</u>мок	*castle*
Зам<u>о</u>к	*lock (with a key or combination)*
<u>О</u>рган	*body organ or government intelligence agency*
Орг<u>а</u>н	*musical instrument often played in churches*

(In the examples above and in the examples that will follow throughout lesson 11, stressed vowels will be <u>underscored</u>.)

When you listened to the sounds of the words in the examples above, you should have heard a difference in the pronunciation of stressed and unstressed vowels. The stressed syllable (underscored vowel) is pronounced for a longer number of milliseconds and the unstressed syllable, not only shorter in length of pronunciation, is also not fully realized according to the pronunciation rules presented in lessons 1-10 above.

Russian has a system of vowel reduction for unstressed vowels. If each number represents a syllable and the number 3 is the stressed syllable, then the number 2 represents a syllable with partial reduction and the number 1 represents a syllable with full reduction. Using this pattern, we could describe the words above with numbers:

Замок	3 – 1	*castle*
Замок	2 – 3	*lock (with a key or combination)*
Орган	3 – 1	*body organ or government intelligence agency*
Орган	2 – 3	*musical instrument often played in churches*

In Russian vowels following the stressed vowel are completely reduced. Vowels preceding the stressed vowel may be partially reduced (if in word initial position) or fully reduced.

Of the 10 Russian vowel letters, 8 (Аа, Яя, Ээ, Ее, Оо, Ёё, Ыы, Ии) are subject to reduction when they are not stressed. The only Russian vowel sounds which are never reduced, even when they are unstressed, are the vowels (Уу, Юю).

In the sections that follow, you will learn about the pronunciation of unstressed vowels in various phonetic contexts.

Reduction of Unstressed *Aa* and *Oo* after Hard Consonants

11.2   Full Reduction of Aa, Oo after Hard Consonants

When either of the Russian vowels Aa or Oo is preceded by a hard consonant (any consonant *except* Чч, Щщ, Йй) and is subject to full reduction, it is pronounced like the vowel in the English words "but" or "dull." This sound is represented in many dictionaries by the symbol "schwa" (ə). You can hear this sound in many English words, such as the following:

A in adept
E in synthesis
I in decimal
O in harmony
U in medium
Y in syringe

(from http://englishplus.com/grammar/00000383.htm accessed May 21, 2004)

In Russian, we pronounce "schwa" for Aa, Oo when either of these vowels is the first syllable of a 3-4 syllable word in which the stress falls on the third syllable, for instance:

(Audio file 11.2 begins here.)

Пропаганда	*propaganda*
Саксофон	*saxophone*

When the vowel sound represented by Aa, Oo in Russian is pronounced as a schwa, this is called "full reduction." There is no way to tell these vowel sounds apart (Aa from Oo) when you hear them: they are the same sound spelled in different ways. In the examples below, the vowel pronounced with a schwa sound is marked in **boldface**.

Reduced Aa (audio file 11.2 resumes here.)

Катар**а**кта	*cataract*
Панор**а**ма	*panorama*
Пара**о**кс	*paradox*

Reduced Oo

М**о**ногр**а**мма	*monogram*
Фот**о**гр**а**фия	*photograph or photography*
Моноп**о**лия	*monopoly (economic concept or game)*

The vowels Aa and Oo are always fully reduced whenever they occur after the stressed vowel, as they do in the words listed below: (Remember, boldface vowels are pronounced like "schwa".)

За**м**ок	*castle*
Орган	*body organ*
Астма	*asthma*
Тр**а**нспорт	*transport, transportation*
Атом	*atom*
Атлас	*atlas*
Б**а**за	*base, basis*
П**а**фос	*pathos*
Д**о**гма	*dogma*
Р**о**бот	*robot*
П**а**спорт	*passport*

11.3   Partial Reduction of Aa, Oo after Hard Consonants

When either Aa or Oo is preceded by a hard consonant and is subject to partial reduction, it is pronounced like the vowel in "hot" or "pot" (American pronunciation only, not British). This type of pronunciation is represented by the number 2 in the "coded diagram" presented in section 11.2 above. We hear partial reduction of these vowels in word-initial position or in a 3-syllable word in the syllable immediatley preceding the stressed vowel. In these examples, italic vowels are partially reduced:

*О*ктаг*о*н	*octagon*
*А*нат*о*мия	*anatomy*
*А*вангард	*avant-garde*

Remember that there is no difference in pronunciation between partially reduced Aa and partially reduced Oo. (Boldfaced vowels are fully reduced, italic vowels are partially reduced.)

Акколада	*accolade*
Аромат	*aromat*
Астроном	*astronomer*
Астролог	*astrologist*
Акрополь	*acropolis*
Автобус	*bus*
Параграф	*paragraph*
Баланс	*balance (noun)*
Гараж	*garage*

Reduction of Unstressed Aa after Soft Consonants

11.4   Partial Reduction of Unstressed Aa after Soft Consonants

The Russian soft-series vowel Яя is generally used with soft consonants, but there are some soft consonants (Чч, Щщ) that cannot be followed by the vowel letter Яя.

After Чч, Щщ the hard-series vowel Aa is written, but the pronunciation of the consonant is still soft. When Aa is unstressed and only partially reduced (if it's in the syllable immediately preceding the stressed syllable), it is pronounced as Ии, as in these examples:

(Remember, boldface vowels are fully reduced, italic vowels are partially reduced.)

Часы	*watch, clock*
Щавель	*sorrel*
Чабан	*shepherd*
Щадить	*to have mercy*
Чанах	*vat for brewing beer*
Щажу	*I will have mercy*
Часа	*a form of the word "hour"*
Щадим	*We will have mercy*
Часов	*a form of the word "hour"*
Щадят	*They will have mercy*

11.5   <u>Full Reduction</u> of Unstressed Аа after Soft Consonants

Whenever Аа follows Чч, Щщ and does not immediately precede the stressed syllable, it is fully reduced. This means that the vowel is pronounced as even shorter and weaker than Ии, as in these examples:

Час<u>а</u>ми	*a form of the word "hour"*
час<u>о</u>в<u>о</u>й	*guard (hourly guard, nightly "watch")*
Чаев<u>ы</u>е	*tip (for a waiter, for example)*
Част<u>и</u>чность	*frequency*
Част<u>у</u>шка	*musical genre (bawdy rhyming couplet)*
Чах<u>о</u>тка	*tuberculosis*
Чайковский	*Tchaikovsky (famous Russian composer)*
Чаров<u>а</u>ть	*to charm, enchant*

Reduction of Unstressed Ее, Яя

11.6   <u>Partial Reduction</u> of Ее, Яя

When either of the vowels Ее, Яя is unstressed, it is also reduced. In partial reduction, in the syllable immediately preceding the stressed syllable or in word-initial position, these vowels are reduced to Ии:

гер<u>о</u>й	*hero*
ляг<u>у</u>шка	*frog*
*Е*вр<u>о</u>па	*Europe*
*Я*нв<u>а</u>рь	*January*
Деф<u>е</u>кт	*defect*
Ге<u>о</u>граф	*geographer*
Пейс<u>а</u>ж	*lanscape*
Ме<u>д</u>бр<u>а</u>т	*male nurse*
Мет<u>а</u>лл	*metal*
Сем<u>е</u>стр	*semester*
Сестр<u>а</u>	*sister*
Вяз<u>а</u>ть	*to knit*
Взял<u>а</u>	*took (past tense)*

11.7   Full Reduction of Ее, Яя

When either of the vowels Ее, Яя is unstressed and more than one syllable away from the stressed syllable, these vowels are pronounced with full reduction. They sound shorter and weaker than the partially reduced vowel Ии:

Вертикаль	*vertical line*
Генерал	*general*
Ветеринар	*veterinarian*
Желатин	*gelatin*
Керосин	*kerosine*
Легион	*legion*
Телефон	*telephone*
Телевизор	*television*
Пессимизм	*pessimism*
Медсестра	*female nurse*
Револьвер	*revolver*
Телеграф	*telegraph*
Сегрегация	*segregation*
Телеграмма	*telegram*

11.8   Full Reduction of Ее, Яя after Another Vowel

When either of the vowels Ее, Яя is unstressed and preceded by another vowel letter, these vowels are pronounced with a y-glide and make a short indeterminate sound similar to the "yuh" sounds in "yuck" or "yummy". There is no difference in pronunciation between Ее and Яя in this context.

Здание	*building*
Здания	*buildings*
Занятие	*Class (university level only)*
Задание	*Assignment*
Задания	*Assignments*
Упражнение	*Exercise*
Упражнения	*Exercises*

Summary Practice

11.9   Practice

The list below consists of geographic place names. The stressed syllable is underscored. Practice
with these placenames and try to identify them in English.

1.   Москв**а**

2.   Пан**а**ма

3.   В**о**логда

4.   Л**о**ндон

5.   Варш**а**ва

6.   **Я**лта

7.   Костром**а**

8.   Кат**а**р

9.   Гав**а**на

10.   Хан**о́**й

11.   Петерб**у**рг

12.   Влад**и**мир

13.   С**у**здаль

14.   Тех**а**с

15.   Чел**я**бинск

16.   Неп**а**л

17.   Сенег**а**л

18.   Ряз**а**нь

19.   Тегер**а**н

20.   К**и**ев

21.   Амстерд**а**м

22.   Нев**а**

23.   Аргент**и**на

24.   Росс**и**я

25.   Яросл**а**вль

26.   Хаб**а**ровск

27.   Ит**а**лия

28.   Португ**а**лия

29.   Исп**а**ния

30.   Финл**я**ндия

31.   Швецария

32.   Украина

33.   Харковь

34.   Англия

35.   Калифорния

11.10   First names

Practice reading out loud these common Russian first names:

Александр, Анна

Борис

Виктория, Вадим. Валерий, Валерия, Владимир

Галина, Георгий

Дмитрий, Дарья

Елена, Екатерина, Елизавета

Алёша, Алёна

Жора, Женя

Зинаида, Зоя

Иван, Ирина, Илья

Константин, Кира, Клавдия, Коля

Лариса, Леонид

Михаил, Мария, Марья

Николай, Наталья, Никита, Нина

Ольга, Олег

Пётр, Павел

Раиса, Родя

Светлана, Софья, Соня

Татьяна, Таня

Фёдор, Федя

Харитон

Шура

Элла

Юлия

Яков, Яша

11.11   Last Names (1)

Practice reading these last names of individuals famous in Russian history and culture. Try to recognize the names and see how many you can identify.

Ахматова, Ахмадулина, Асанова, Аксёнов, Андропов

Бухарин, Бродский, Брежнев, Булгаков, Барышников

Венедиктов, Введенский, Верещагин, Виноградов, Войнович

Гоголь, Глинка, Гиппиус, Гагарин, Глазунов, Гайдар, Горбачёв

Достоевский, Дмитрий Донской

Есенин, Евтушенко, Ежов, Ельцин

11.12   Last Names (2)

Practice reading these last names of individuals famous in Russian history and culture. Try to recognize the names and see how many you can identify.

Жуковский, Жданов, Жуков

Зиновьев, Заболоцкий, Замятин, Зощенко

Иван Грозный

Кондратьев, Кандинский, Каменев, Каспаров

Ломоносов, Лермонтов, Лесков, Ленин, Лихачёв

Мусоргский, Менделеев, Маяковский, Мандельштам, Мейерхольд, Малевич

11.13   Last Names (3)

Practice reading these last names of individuals famous in Russian history and culture. Try to recognize the names and see how many you can identify.

Александр Невский, Набоков, Некрасов, Нечаев

Оболенский, Ожегов, Одоевский, Олеша, Островский

Пушкин, Петрушевская, Прокофьев, Павлов, Павлова, Путин

Романов, Распутин, Радищев, Разин, Рахманинов, Ремизов, Репин, Рождественский

11.14 Last Names (4)

Practice reading these last names of individuals famous in Russian history and culture. Try to recognize the names and see how many you can identify.

Столыпин, Стравинский, Сталин, Синявский, Солженицын, Сахаров

Толстой, Тургенев, Третьяков, Троцкий, Терешкова, Толстая, Тарковский, Токарева

Ульянов, Успенский, Ушаков

Фёдоров, Фадеев, Флоренский, Фонвизин,

11.15 Last Names (5)

Practice reading these last names of individuals famous in Russian history and culture. Try to recognize the names and see how many you can identify.

Хлебников, Ходасевич, Хомяков, Хачатурян, Хрущёв

Цветаева, Цветков,

Чайковский, Чаадаев, Чехов, Чернышевский, Чуковский, Чуковская, Черненко

11.16 Last Names (6)

Practice reading these last names of individuals famous in Russian history and culture. Try to recognize the names and see how many you can identify.

Шолохов, Шагал, Шварц, Шереметьев, Шестов, Шукшин, Шостакович,

Щедрин, Щербаков, Щукин,

Эйзенштейн, Эрдман

Юсупов

Ягода

Self-Quiz

11.17   Self-Quiz

Listen to the words on the tape and mark the stress in this list. Try to identify the placenames in English!

1.	Япония	11.	Багдад
2.	Германия	12.	Парагвай
3.	Детройт	13.	Осло
4.	Галифакс	14.	Марокко
5.	Египет	15.	Кострома
6.	Канада	16.	Волгоград
7.	Торонто	17.	Ямайка
8.	Айова	18.	Орегон
9.	Висконсин	19.	Оренбург
10.	Миннесота	20.	Находка

Appendix

Hard Consonants
There are three Russian consonants that are *always hard:*

Ж, Ц, Ш

Soft Consonants
There are three Russian consonants that are *always soft:*

Й, Ч, Щ

Hard-Series Vowels
There are five Russian hard-series vowels:

а, о, у, ы, э

Soft-Series Vowels
There are five Russian soft-series vowels:

е, ё, и, ю, я

All of these vowels have y-glides when word initial or when preceded by another vowel
EXCEPT И.

Voiced Consonants
The following Russian consonants are voiced consonants. When in word-final position, they are pronounced like their voiceless mate (in parentheses) if they have one.

б (п), в (ф), г (к), д (т), ж (ш), з (с), л, м, н, р

Voiceless Consonants
The following Russian consonants are voiceless consonants. Letters in parentheses are the voiceless consonants' voiced mates. When followed by a voiced consonant, the voiceless consonant is pronounced like its voiced mate. Exceptions to this rule are the following sound combinations: сл, см, сн, св, ср

к (г), п (б), с (з), т (д), ф (в), х, ц, ч, ш (ж), щ

Charts of Russian Letters

1. Hard- and Soft-Series Vowels

Hard-Series Vowels	Soft-Series Vowels
А	Я
У	Ю
Э	Е
О	Ё
Ы	*И

*the only soft-series vowel without a y-glide

2. Hard and Soft Consonants

Consonants: Always Hard	Consonants: Hard or Soft	Consonants: Always Soft
Ж, Ц, Ш	Б, В, Г, Д, З, К, Л, М, Н, П, Р, С, Т, Ф, Х	Й, Ч, Щ

Consonants in the middle column of the chart directly above are soft if they are followed by a soft-consonant, a soft-series vowel, or the soft-sign. Otherwise, they are hard.

3. Voiced and Voiceless Consonants

Voiced Consonants	Voiceless Consonants
Б	П
В	Ф
Г	К
Д	Т
Ж	Ш
З	С
Л	
М	
Н	
Р	
	Х
	Ц
	Ч
	Щ

Letters appearing in the same row are mates. Letters without a mate are unpaired.

Spelling Rules

There are three basic spelling rules in Russian:

1.   **After** any one of the following letters

к, г, х, ж, ч, ш, щ

*Never write **ы**, but always **и**.*

2.   **After** any one of the following letters

ж, ц, ч, ш, щ

*Never write unstressed **о**. Always write **е** instead.*

3.   **After** any one of the four hushers

ж, ч, ш, щ

*Never write **я** or **ю**, always write **а** or **у** instead.*

Alphabetical Order

Review alphabetical order by reading through the letters in the alphabet three times:

Аа Бб Вв Гг Дд Ее Ёё Жж Зз Ии Йй Кк Лл Мм Нн Оо Пп
Рр Сс Тт Уу Фф Хх Цц Чч Шш Щщ Ъъ Ыы Ьь Ээ Юю Яя

Аа Бб Вв Гг Дд Ее Ёё Жж Зз Ии Йй Кк Лл Мм Нн Оо Пп
Рр Сс Тт Уу Фф Хх Цц Чч Шш Щщ Ъъ Ыы Ьь Ээ Юю Яя

Аа Бб Вв Гг Дд Ее Ёё Жж Зз Ии Йй Кк Лл Мм
Нн Оо ПпРр Сс Тт Уу Фф Хх Цц Чч Шш Щщ
Ъъ Ыы Ьь Ээ Юю Яя

Now consider these mnenomic devices:

A **b**ig **V**alentine **g**ets **d**irty **e**asily. (абвгде)

Your **t**reasure-**z**enith **i**s a **y**ellow **k**itten's **l**ove. (ёжзийкл)

Michael **n**ever **o**vercooks **p**enne **r**igata. (мнопр)

Susan **t**ries (**u**sually) **f**our **x**-rays. (стуфх)

It's a **s**harp **f**resh **ch**eese: **hard**-**y** but **soft**. (цчшщъыь)

Ellen! **You** have bought a **y**acht! (эюя)

Towards the end of the alphabet, remember that there is a nearly perfect alternation of hard and soft consonants and other letters, with hard always preceding soft:

Hard	ц
Soft	ч
Hard	ш
Soft	щ
Hard Sign	ъ
(Hard-series vowel)	ы
Soft Sign	ь
Hard-series vowel	э
Soft-series vowel	ю

The alphabet ends with the letter that means "I" (я), the first-person personal pronoun, because in Russian "I" is always the last person in the list. (This word is not capitalized in Russian, unless it is sentence-initial.)